ARTe OF NOW:
PRACTICE OF IMMEDIACY IN THE ARTS™

Dearest Patricia (Choe)
what a gift you are!
I'm so happy to share
PIA with you, enjoy!
Big hug & lots of love,
Nicole
3-9-17

SINGING HORSE PRESS 2017

When bringing the full expression of yourself as a creator into the flow of every moment, the voices of the critical mind are usually the loudest. In Nicolee McMahon's new book, she uses *Arte of Now: Practice of Immediacy in the Arts*™, "PIA," as the modality to get into the creative flow. Her clarity of description in how to make your emotions, feelings and experiences in the moment part of the process, is Zen awareness. Going with the flow compassionately will be a central role in your ability to make and refine not just your art but your life.

Stephanie Goldman, Fine Artist, Instructor, Author
and Secretary-National Watercolor Society.

The creative moment is wide open to anyone willing to trust the process Nicolee McMahon describes in her illuminating book *Arte of Now: Practice of Immediacy in the Arts*.™ An experiential method developed by McMahon, the practice of immediacy seems well suited for students of the arts to explore the "moment of Now" as they deepen their creative instincts and intuition.

Sandra Fluck, Founder of bookscover2cover.com

ARTE OF NOW:
PRACTICE OF IMMEDIACY IN THE ARTS™

NICOLEE MCMAHON

Cover Image: 'Wings' PIA acrylic on canvas, Nicolee McMahon

ISBN 978-0-935162-81-3

Arte of Now: Practice of Immediacy in the Arts ™ is available directly from the author at www.practiceofimmediacy.com and from Small Press Distribution at spdbooks.org.

Singing Horse Press
12170 Ragweed Street
San Diego, CA 92129

Acknowledgements

"Tell me, what is it you plan to do
with your one wild and precious life?"

from "The Summer Day"
by poet Mary Oliver

My response: I decided to do what felt impossible, write the *Arte of Now: Practice of Immediacy in the Arts.*™ Yet, I've been supported at every turn and I'd like to acknowledge the people who helped bring this project to fruition. Paul Naylor, my publisher, an accomplished poet, guided me with his big generous heart and spirit. My husband Barry, who has my back and wants the best for me and others, listened and edited whenever I needed his input. To my children Dana and Tyson whose comments were so lovingly helpful, including Tyson's prodding me to go beyond what I thought I could do. To Annie Pirruccello, who has taught the *Practice of Immediacy in the Arts* so skillfully for years and helped me craft words when I was at a loss. To Robert Althouse, Joan Hoeberichts, Annie Pirruccello, and Vivienne Lund for their featured work in *Arte of Now*. To Wendy, Stephanie, Ken and Sandy for their wonderful, thoughtful blurbs on the back and front inside. And to the many people who read the book and gave me such invaluable input: Robert Althouse, Sara Bridges, Nancy Burnett, Sandy Fluck, Steven Gelb, Ken and Stephanie Goldman, Kelly Harrington, Lisa Lanzetta, Catherine Pages Roshi, Frances Pope, and Patrece Powers. And for the transformative teaching and guidance of my Zen Teacher, Taizan Maezumi Roshi, thank you. With deep gratitude for the many years of support Genpo Merzel Roshi and Hal and Sidra Stone have given me.

To those present now and to the generations
to come—may your creativity flourish

Contents

Introduction

Arte of Now explores the wisdom of creativity through a particular lens called the *Practice of Immediacy in the Arts®* (PIA). My background as a Zen teacher who has been engaged in the arts since childhood prepared the soil in which PIA could grow. What has emerged is a way of being creative that is inclusive and not bound by interior restraints—such as the inner judge, critic, or perfectionist. Instead of suppressing or identifying with these inner aspects of yourself, PIA includes them as part of the creative process, along with whatever else has come into awareness from your outer environment. As you practice with PIA, "inner" and "outer" dissolve, and you learn to include the many forms that enter your awareness.

"PIA" is expressed in two different ways: Pure PIA and revised PIA (PIA+). Pure PIA is not preplanned: you have no idea what you are going to create, and you complete it in one sitting, never to be worked on again. I have represented pure PIA through visual art in Part Two. Part One includes the history and philosophy of PIA as well as the *voice of PIA* poem. Directions for PIA are detailed in Part Three. Revised PIA (PIA+) are visual art pieces that originated with pure PIA, but they have been thought about and worked on at a later time. Thus, this work no longer follows the directions for PIA. Revised PIA can be found in Part Four, and it is represented through visual art pieces. I have also included one poem in revised PIA. Part Five concludes *Arte of Now*.

To truly get a feel for pure PIA, please watch one or several abbreviated videos of pure PIA at http://practiceofimmediacy.com/pia-videos.

Part One:

Practice of Immediacy in the Arts

The way the self arrays itself is the form of the entire world. See each thing in this entire world as a moment of time. Things do not hinder one another, just as moments do not hinder one another. The way-seeking mind arises in this moment. A way-seeking moment arises in this mind. It is the same with practice and attaining the way. Thus the self setting itself out in array sees itself. This is the understanding that the self is time. . . . Each moment is all being, is the entire world. Reflect now whether any being or any world is left out of the present moment.

Dogen Zenji, from a section of "Uji" (Being-Time) *Shobogenzo*
(*Moon in a Dewdrop*, edited by Kazuaki Tanahashi)

Philosophy of PIA

Arte of Now: Practice of Immediacy in the Arts™ is an experiential practice in which one opens to *not knowing*—an open and nonjudgmental mind space that lets go of opinions, views, concepts and desired outcomes. Not knowing neither grasps nor rejects anything, but instead includes whatever arises. As Dogen says, "Things do not hinder one another, just as moments do not hinder one another."

This is why initially it may be helpful to think of PIA as an awareness practice of opening to whatever is happening: a feeling of boundless elation, resistance, the smell of compost, a tiny ant navigating the rim of one's glasses, a loud car horn, a judgment about PIA. No matter what arises, we neither hold on to nor repress it: "Each moment is all being, is the entire world."

However, PIA involves expressing this moment through writing, music, movement, painting, sketching, ipad/computer, scuplting, woodworking, dance or other creative media. At the end of the PIA session, what you have created is not the expression of a preconceived plan but of "not knowing" in action. This form of practice requires the same attention and commitment as other awareness modalities. By trusting the process and practicing with including everything, an innate spaciousness and a creative flow can emerge.

Leaving nothing out is a deep part of meditative experience that allows us to realize the interrelated unity of everything. Seeing this oneness, we realize that nothing is missing, and the uniqueness of each moment is inherently equal to the next. Consider that, in current calculations, our earth is moving at 30 kilometers per second around the sun, while the solar system is moving at 220 kilometers per second around our galaxy, which is moving within a cluster of galaxies at 1,000 kilometers per second in an expanding universe. With this enormous speed and constant change, one can see that all forms are changing every nano second, and they will never be repeated in exactly the same way. The visual depictions of our universe in pictures and films allow us to grasp, through our own perception, the interrelated fabric of the world and our lives. We are so fortunate to live in a time where the intersection of science and deep mystical experience can help us understand Dogen's words: "Reflect now whether any being or any world is left out of the present moment."

The experience of PIA can make more concrete the ever-changing nature of our world and help us open to what is at hand. For example, when PIA is practiced by someone in the arts who is stuck and not able to move forward, you include the "stuckness" by giving form to it in the medium you have chosen. The same is true for resistance or whatever else is blocking or restricting creativity. In other words, these things become part of what is being expressed creatively. It does not matter whether what is arising is coming from within us or from our environment, it's all included. "The way the self arrays itself is the form of the entire world."

Applying the Practice

What follows are descriptions of three different people applying the 5 simple directions below for giving form to PIA (more detailed guidance is in Part Three, the "How To Do PIA" section of this book):

1. Select media you want to work with
2. Open to not knowing
3. Include and express what you are aware of as it shows up
4. Express expectations as they are occurring
5. If you enter a creative flow, follow its unfolding

The late musician Nate Manning used PIA to move through his own creative block:

> I'm a musician and I have struggled with creative flow for nine years. . . . Just when I thought I was going to give up creativity I discovered PIA. At first I didn't get it . . . but then the light turned on. An intense flow entered me and I became completely at peace with the chaos. My fingers moved and after a while there was nothing more to express from the senses through my fingers. I hit a creative flow and I began to play. I felt like a little kid painting the room with sound. There was nothing to create, nowhere to get to, nothing to worry about. I was here. I continue to use this practice daily in my music. It helps me create art. . . . For me, PIA is a process that helps me be open to everything inside and out and keep the flow of life moving constant in my awareness.

Annie Pirruccello Sensei, a Zen teacher who has been practicing and teaching PIA for many years, said that

> Using art media to express what is right here, right now, I slow down and deeply experience life, including what often passes quickly and with minimal awareness. PIA seems particularly helpful in opening to what is unpleasant or unexciting, and magnifies experiences that are so subtle as to be overshadowed by more energetic ones. Nothing is taboo or too unimportant to express: an undercurrent of fear, red-tailed hawks vocalizing, the wind blowing through the branches of a four hundred year-old oak. While it is true that all of this is available no matter what I am doing, there is something about PIA that throws things into higher relief and deeper intimacy. And I feel another kind of relief too, the kind that comes with realizing that I

> don't have to hide from anything that life presents. My own actions or those of others, words, objects, situations, relationships, nature—I am free to be all of these. But if I want to run from them, to run from who I am and find only separation, I am perfectly free to do that too.

Artist and Zen teacher Robert Althouse Roshi, who works with digital media on his iPad and computer, describes his experience of PIA:

> Staying open to the chaos is interesting. It's like maintaining an active gaze and completely letting go of control/knowing. And then, yes, I get into some kind of flow with the whole thing and it comes together magically.

When practicing with PIA, I have no idea what will be created. PIA has enabled me to give form to images I would otherwise not have thought to express. I feel in my body when a painting is finished. I stand back and am often amazed at what has emerged. When practicing with PIA in writing or painting with acrylics and other media, I'm including everything I'm aware of. Yet selection of what is in the foreground is happening because the media and instruments can't keep up with the flow of awareness. What gets onto the canvas or paper is what I'm most aware of until a creative flow occurs; then the media, instruments, attention are all together flowing. What emerges can be completely surprising. Often the piece is a messy expression of Now. Regardless of whether I finish a piece or it remains a messy experience of opening to the moment, I often begin with a pattern of contraction that shows up as resistance, judgments, dismissing. I include it by giving color, shape, words, movement to whatever the form of tightness that is arising, as well as giving form to a car going by, prickly sensations, a bird chirping, dismissive thoughts, the sound of water running, curiosity, a door slamming shut . . . In other words, I begin fluidly giving form to what's happening Now. When I'm done, the moment is layered before me. In the end, PIA can be fun, and the creative part of me is satisfied to be expressive in this way.

History of PIA

You may be interested in learning how PIA came about. My longstanding exploration of art, along with Zen training, prepared the ground. In the mid-1990s, while on a 5 day retreat with Vipassana teacher Jack Kornfield and Stan Grof, the developer of holotropic breath work, I participated in a holotropic breath session and had an unusual experience when all of my energy systems lined up. I felt as if the top of my head opened and powerful creative energy entered, passed through my body, was born out the other end of my torso, immediately encircling the world. The memory of the experience is as vivid now as it was then. I had no idea what it meant, but it felt like a transmission that needed to be shared. Had the experience not been so visceral, doubt may have swallowed the wonder of it and turned it into grey ash. All I knew was that a creative energy that I did not understand was suddenly taking life in this world, my world. My body knew something my head could not sift through. Something had been born, and I clearly knew I was entrusted with taking care of it. But how?

In time, a knowing began to emerge. My logical, practical mind hid the experience from everyone but a few—I felt it was too strange for people to accept. Although I did PIA in my home studio, the fear of introducing PIA into Zen retreats and of being judged for doing so engulfed me for several years. It was as if I were crossing a line and breaking a taboo I was carrying about Zen that did not include PIA in a retreat. Yet it was while practicing PIA with a variety of materials during a week-long retreat that the overwhelming fear showed up, and what unfolded was a structure with eyes staring down hard on a meditation hall scene. Following a creative flow, I added a goofy figure with rotating yellow and blue eyes looking around the wall of the meditation room, and the spell was broken.

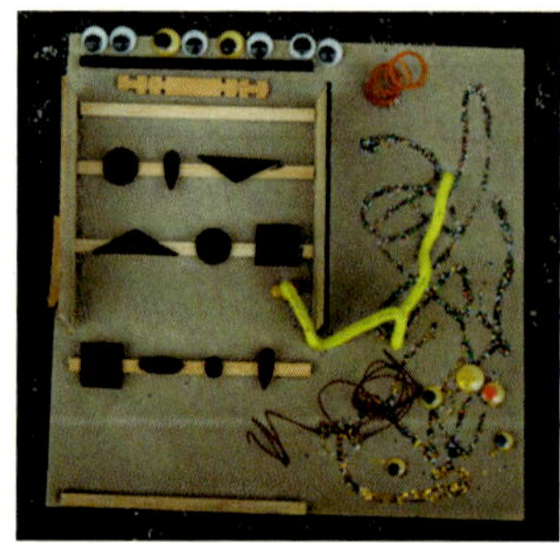

PIA had slipped through my self imposed "follow the rules" barrier and could now live in the open. At first I called this creative energy "spontaneous expression," then the "practice of immediacy," and now I call it *Arte of Now,* with the subtitle of *Practice of Immediacy in the Arts®* (PIA). I added a small "e" to the English word for "Art" to remind us to include everything. As Dogen wrote, "See each thing in this entire world as a moment of time."

Although PIA was now in the open and I was learning to follow creative flow wherever it might lead, I wanted to learn more about this creative energy. I am trained in a method called Voice Dialogue, a psycho-spiritual tool developed by my mentors Hal and Sidra Stone, and I wanted to try it with PIA. I felt it could help me access this creative energy at a deeper level. Using my Voice Dialogue training, I was able to get in touch with the different "internal voices." Each voice is a different energetic state of perception, such as my "inner critic," my "vulnerable part," my "controller," or my "pusher" (that pushes action). We all have many different aspects of ourselves, and using Voice Dialogue, I could access and give voice to them. I now wanted to try this practice to hear the *voice of PIA* speaking for itself without other filters. So, many years ago, on two different days, I got a piece of paper and a pencil, shifted to the *voice of PIA*, and let *PIA* speak for itself. (Note: Practice of Immediacy in the Arts does not require any knowledge of Voice Dialogue.)

First day:

I flow through all media expressing fleeting moments of Now that can't be grasped ---------gone
each moment of time dissolved, only a shadow can ever be seen
a moment here or there, a cut of wood, a guitar string becomes an airplane's roar.
The whole universe is my playground
expand beyond your horizons
let awareness fill the page with sounds, shapes, color, words
in syntax, out of syntax, scribbled letters of all different sizes and shapes....
and if a creative flow emerges, follow it, surf the waves(s), not knowing
where they take your writing instrument.
Space is filled with forms, forms are full of space.
The room you are in is mainly space—include space.
Wherever awareness perceives/alights.....just that
in color/sound/shape/form/words/beads/wood/clay/movement ....
however your media and awareness flow: not two and two.
Everything included.
Every moment equal to the next.
Timeless, formless...... taking shape as form in time.
Who knows what will emerge.
Trust..faith..awareness..opening..not knowing
bearing witness to the cacophony of Now.
An ephemeral moment, never to be repeated.....eternal.
I'm the immediacy of experience flowing through creative forms.

I'm awareness, I shift between sensations, emotion, airplanes, laughter, perception, refrigerator motor, clocks—judgment, confusion, toilet flushing, flowing........
sometimes moving fast, sometimes slow, sometimes not moving at all.
The end......for now

Second day:

I'm full of possibility, I can change direction at any time and am not bound by antiquated ideas of how to produce art.
I'm awareness practice that's alive, vital, active.
I'm not limited by being stiff. I like to engage with all that 'is' in my environment.
I'm fun, playful, scared, dark, depressed—moods go up and down.
I'm the earth and her creatures and their creations, making sounds grrrrr, bzzzzz, shhmr
I move like wind and follow what captures my attention giving shape, form, color (sometimes)
to the unknown mystery that emerges in each fleeting, infinite moment.
I'm not held back by fear, flow, outcome
I play in the flowing, limitless field of Now.
Sometimes choosing a color to plop on the paper/canvas is where to begin
plop, plop someone is walking across the floor.
Starting with colors you're drawn to squirt some on a tray then express the emerging moment.
Inside or outside makes no difference, include what unfolds.
^^^^^^^======__________^^^^^^^^^^ -------
If awareness is speeding along
if awareness is slower and more specific, that too.
Fear—what color, shape is it?

Include the color/line/shape of repressing too.
The field of infinity is vast, boundless, boundlessly inclusive.
Include whatever 'self' ideas emerge (self-judgment, opinions, concepts)
scribble them any place and any size on the canvas/paper.
If you limit yourself, compare, compete—give color/line/form/sound/
movement to that too.
The outcome is not the piece, it's you.
You are teaching yourself to open wide, to dance.
When a creative flow is present, follow it......enjoy.
When it's done, is another surface ready
to capture the unfiltered moment?
No matter what media, these are snapshots of Now.

I was very moved by the *voice of PIA* using the Voice Dialogue technique. I felt somewhat like a parent hearing the first expressions of her child, and I found the words that had come forth to be deep, grounding, clear and playful. I have struggled to find words about the practice of immediacy that would make sense to others and have found it easier to visually show others PIA in action. The words of the *voice of PIA* captured what I had not been able to articulate. For that reason, I decided to pair the above stanzas with visual art in a more direct and accessible way by using words and images together in Part Two. I have maintained the sequence of the *voice of PIA* poem as it appears above, but I have broken it into smaller stanzas in order to accompany the art works. May you enjoy what follows, and may you engage with the open field of possibility of *Arte of Now: the Practice of Immediacy in the Arts.*™

PART TWO:

PRACTICE OF IMMEDIACY IN THE ARTS (PIA)—VISUAL EXAMPLES

I flow through all media
expressing
fleeting moments of Now
that can't be grasped
---------gone
each moment of time
dissolved,

Opposite page: 'Light' PIA acrylic on canvas, Nicolee

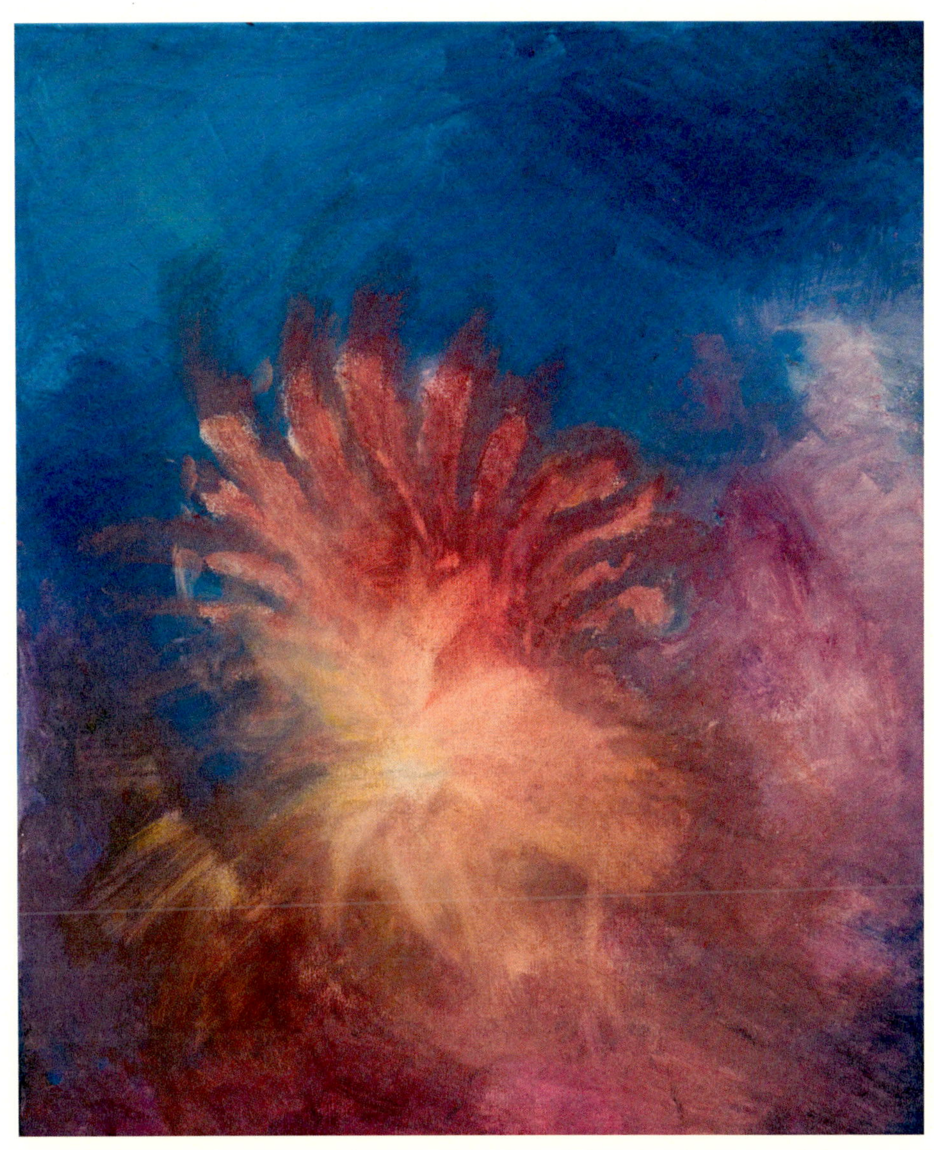

only a shadow can ever be seen
— a moment here or there,

Opposite page: 'PI' PIA acrylic on canvas, Nicolee

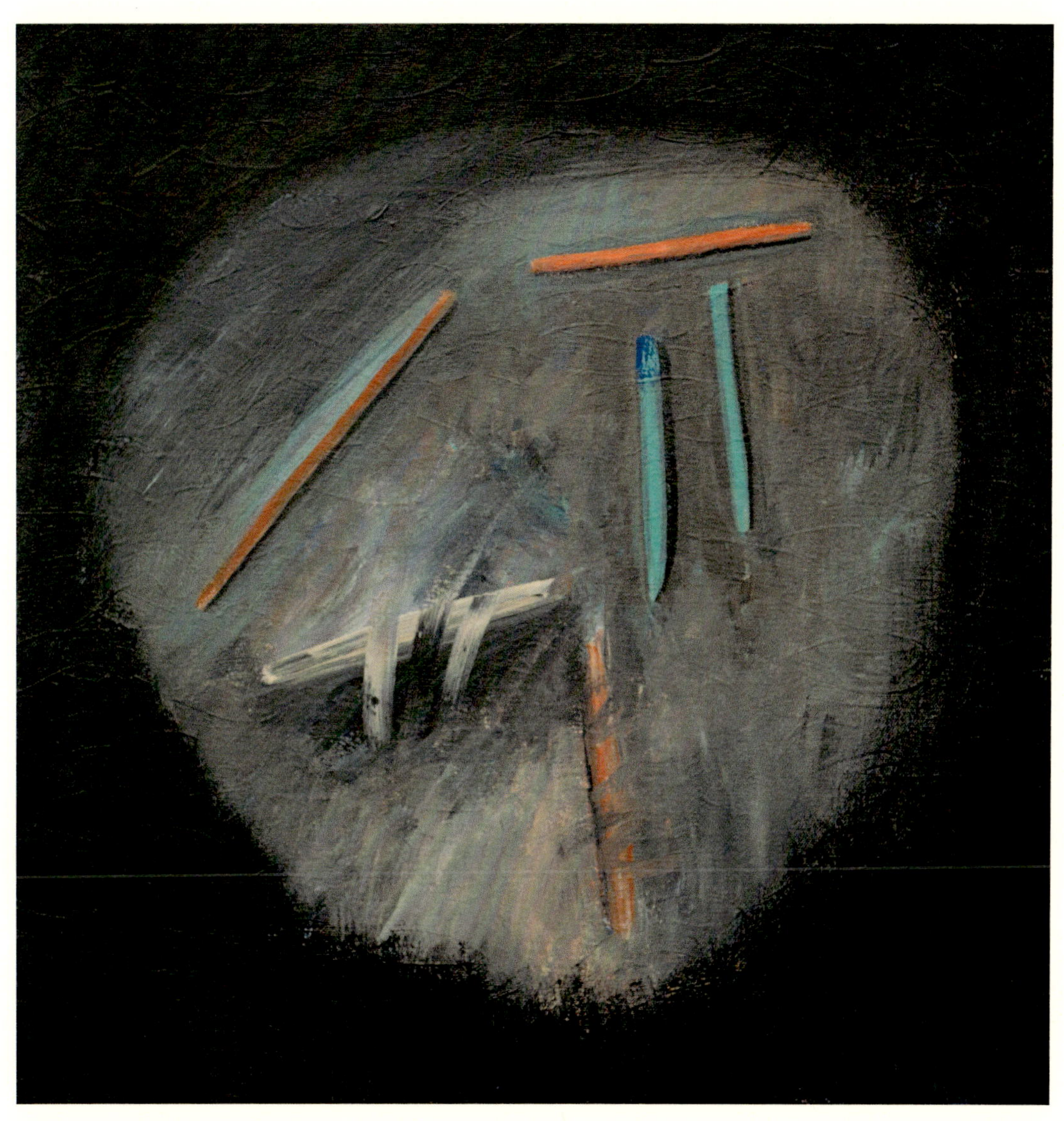

a cut of wood, a guitar string
becomes an airplane's roar.

Opposite page: 'Popeye Swallows the Universe' PIA acrylic on canvas board, Nicolee

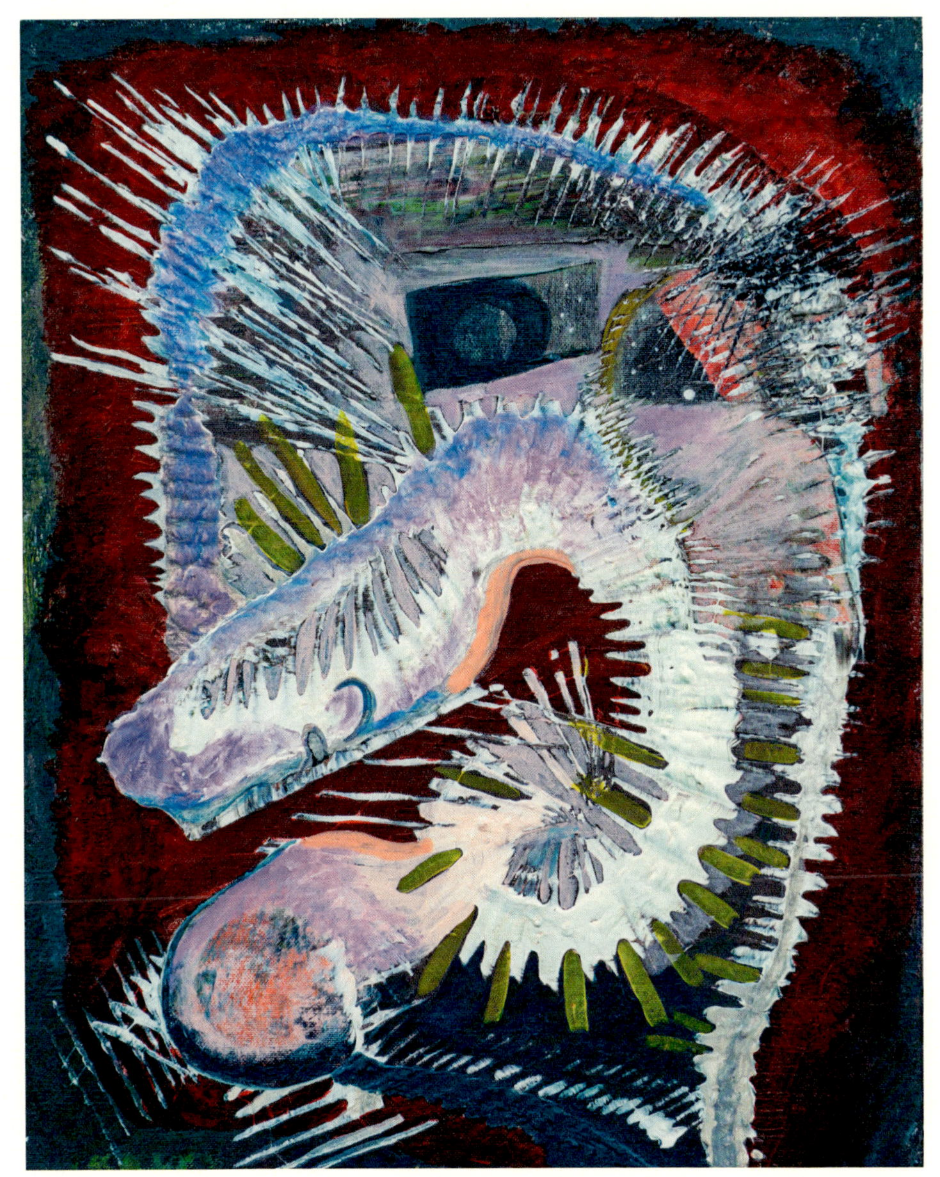

The whole universe is my playground

Opposite page: 'Star Eye' PIA, oil pastel on paper, Nicolee

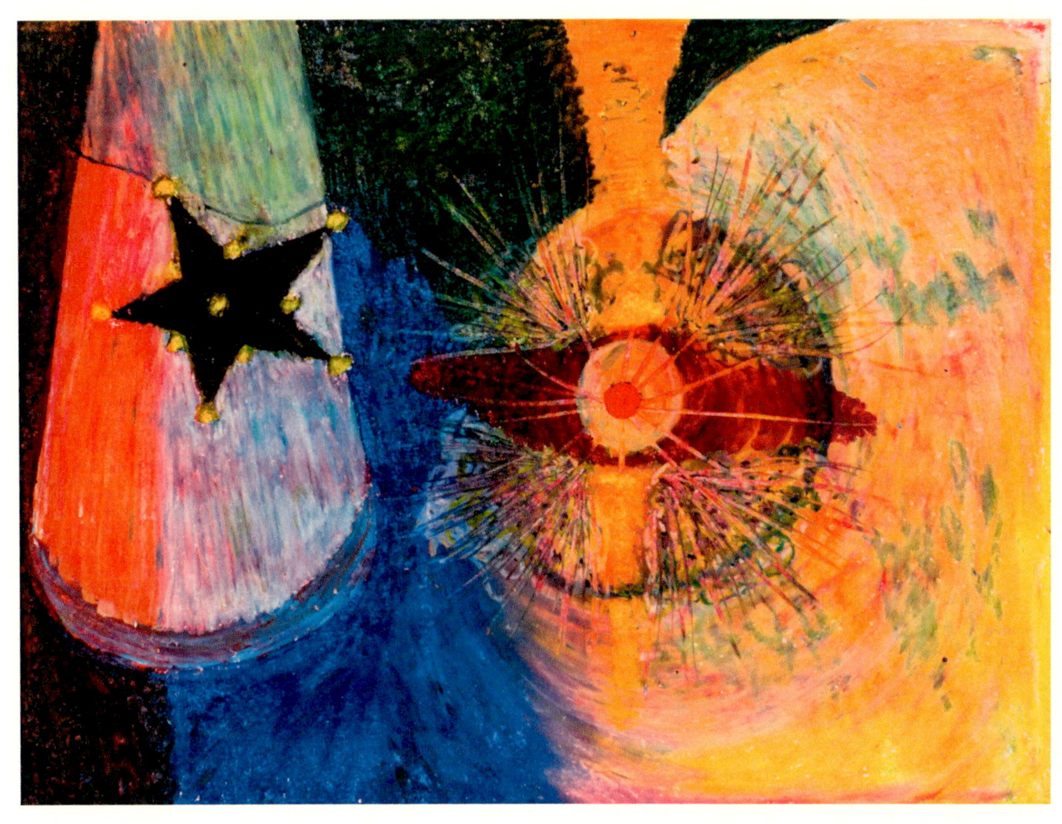

expand beyond your horizons
let awareness fill the page with sounds,
shapes, color, words in syntax,
out of syntax, scribbled letters
of all different sizes and shapes.....

Opposite page: 'What's Happening Now' PIA pastels on canvas, Annie Pirruccello

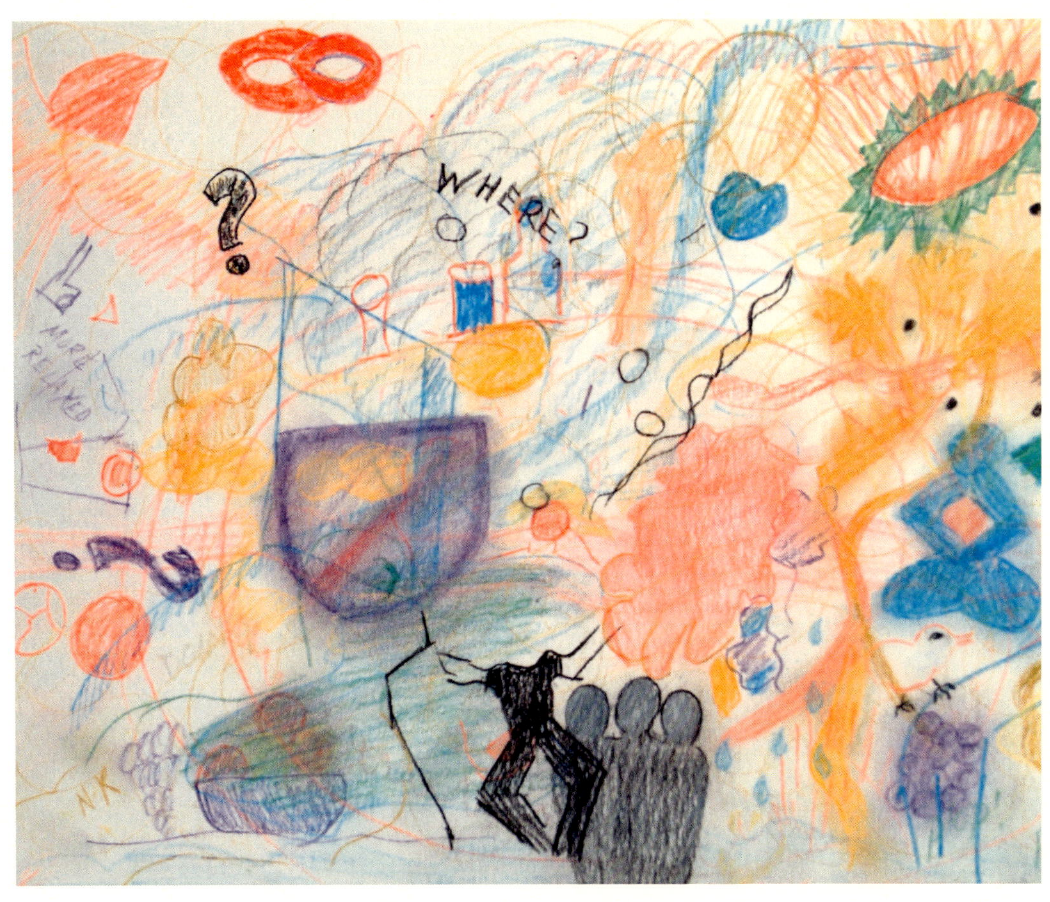
WHERE?

and if
a creative flow
emerges,
follow it,
surf the waves(s),
not knowing
where they take
your writing instrument

Opposite page: 'Word Fence' PIA, acrylic on plexiglass, Nicolee

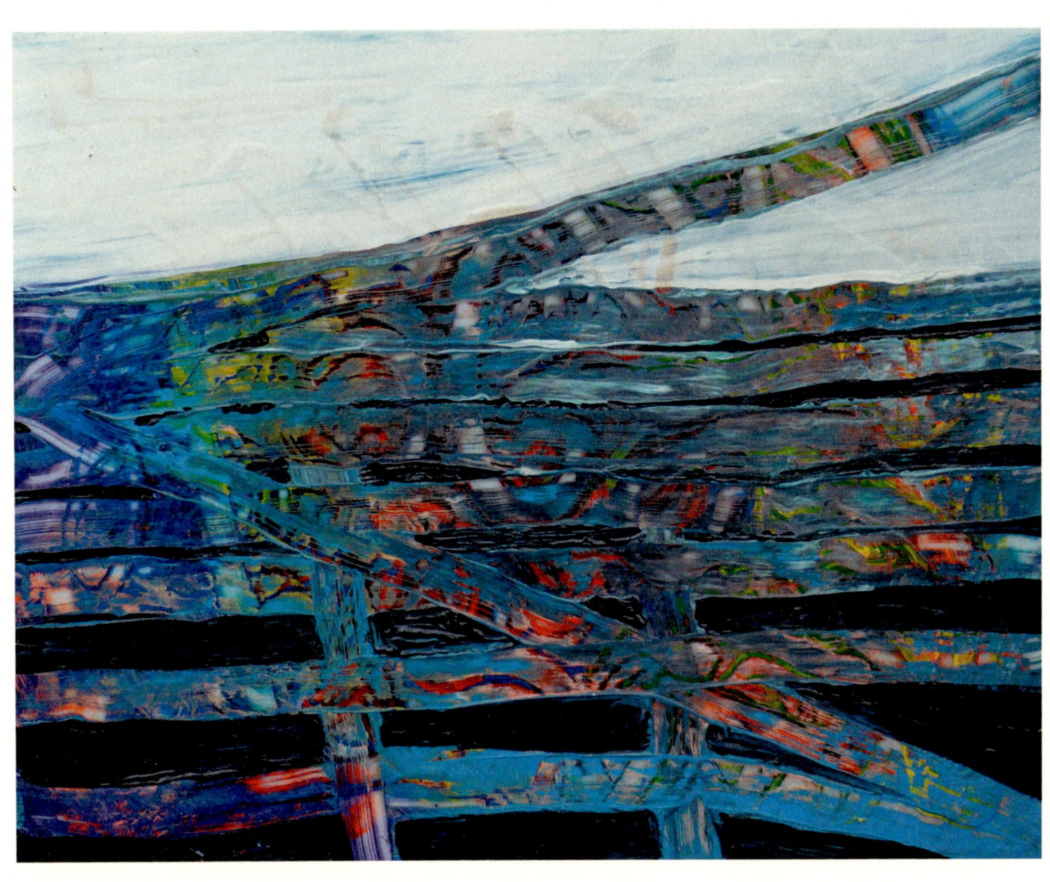

Space is filled with forms,
forms are full of space.
The room you are in
is mainly space—
include space.

Opposite page: 'Dancing Paper' PIA acrylic, paper on canvas, Nicolee

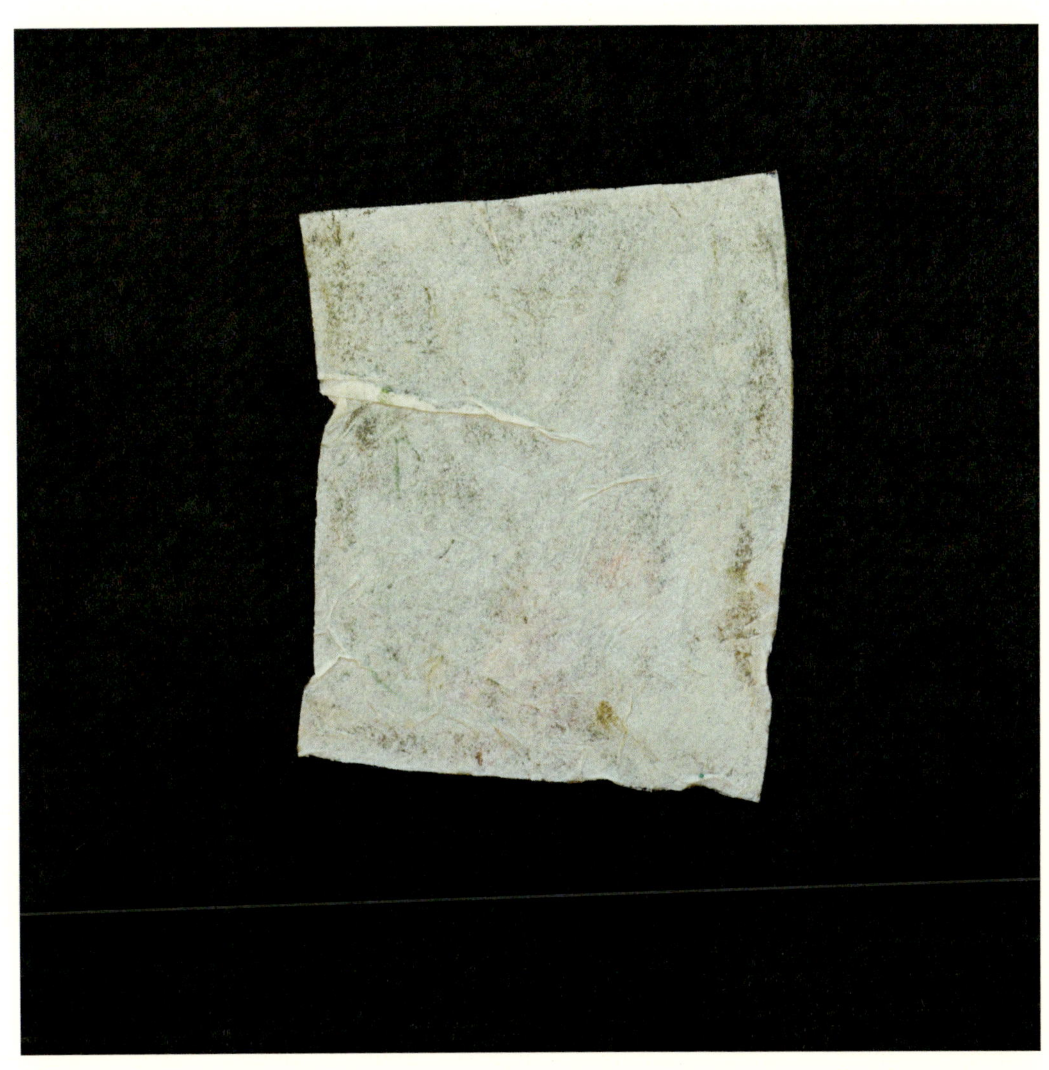

Wherever awareness perceives/alights.....just that

Opposite page: 'A Way Through' PIA acrylic on canvas, Nicolee

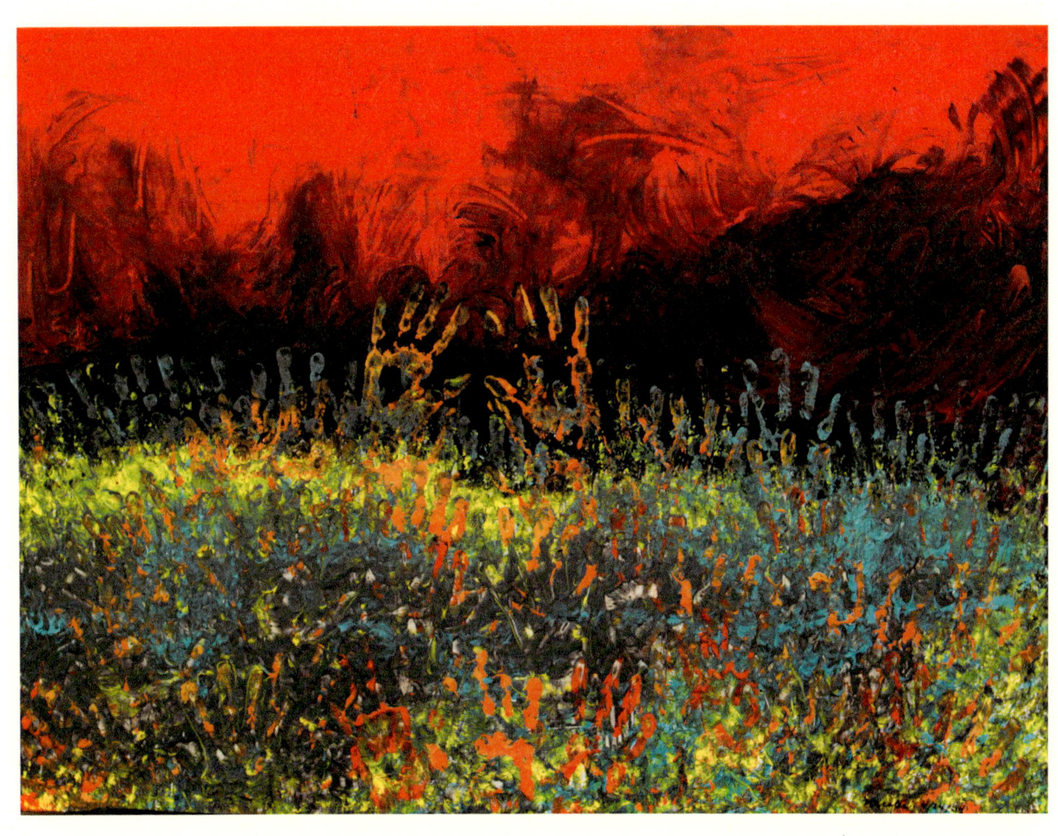

in color / sound / shape /
form / words / beads /
wood / clay / movement ....
however your media and
awareness flow:
not two and two.

Opposite page: 'Wings' PIA acrylic on canvas, Nicolee

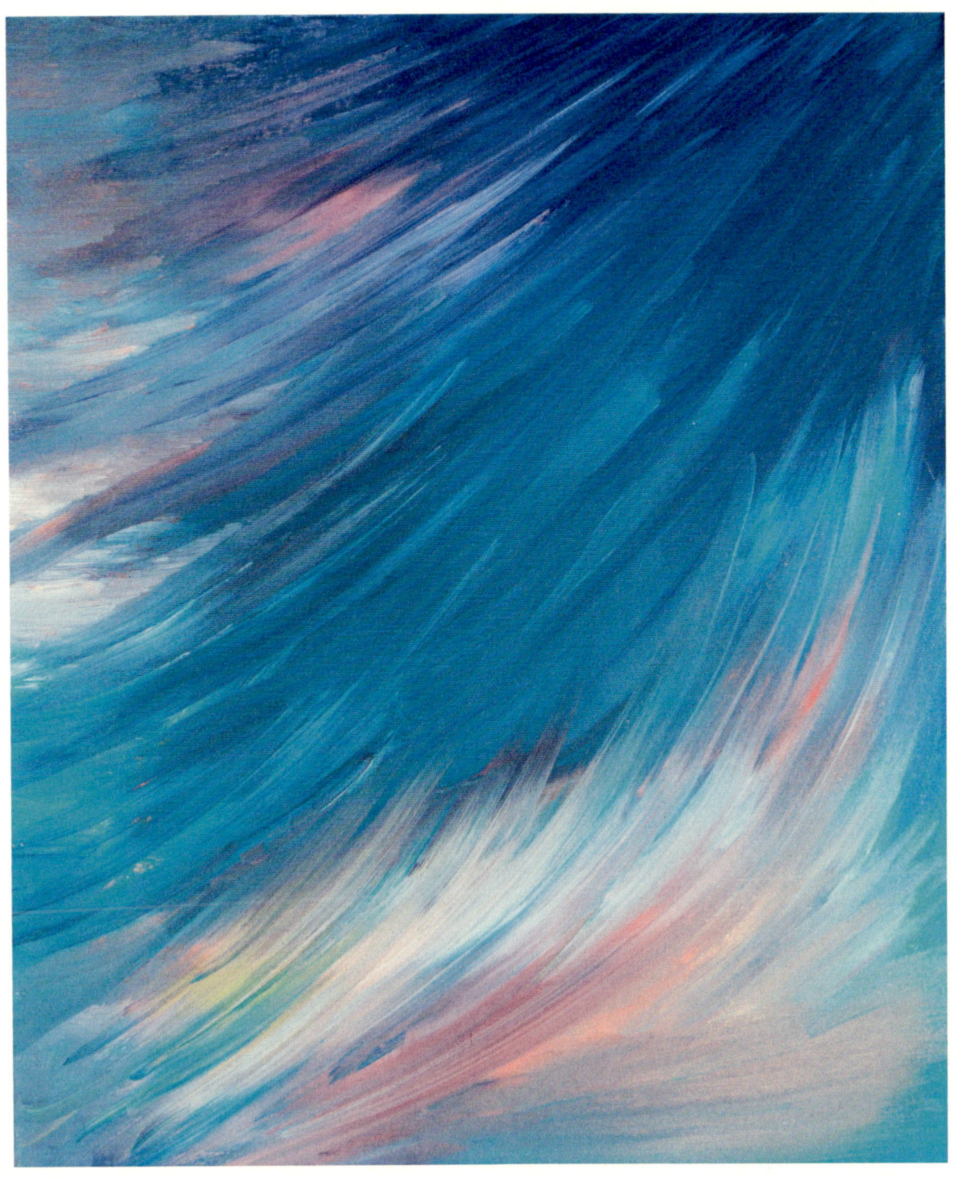

Everything included.
Every moment
equal to the next.

Opposite page: 'Promise to Mother Earth' PIA acrylic on canvas, Nicolee

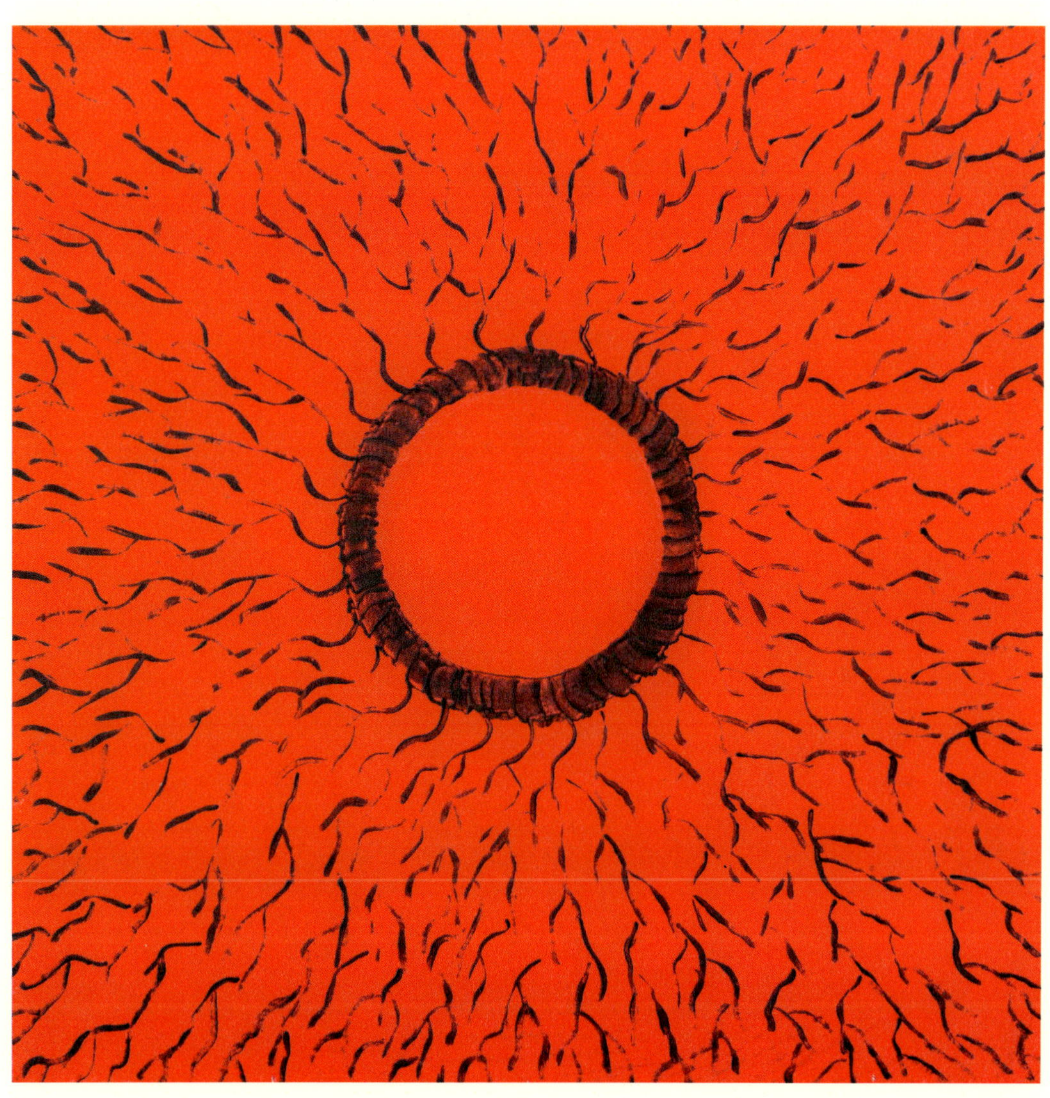

Timeless,
formless......
taking shape
as form in time.

Opposite page: 'Birth' PIA acrylic on canvas, Nicolee

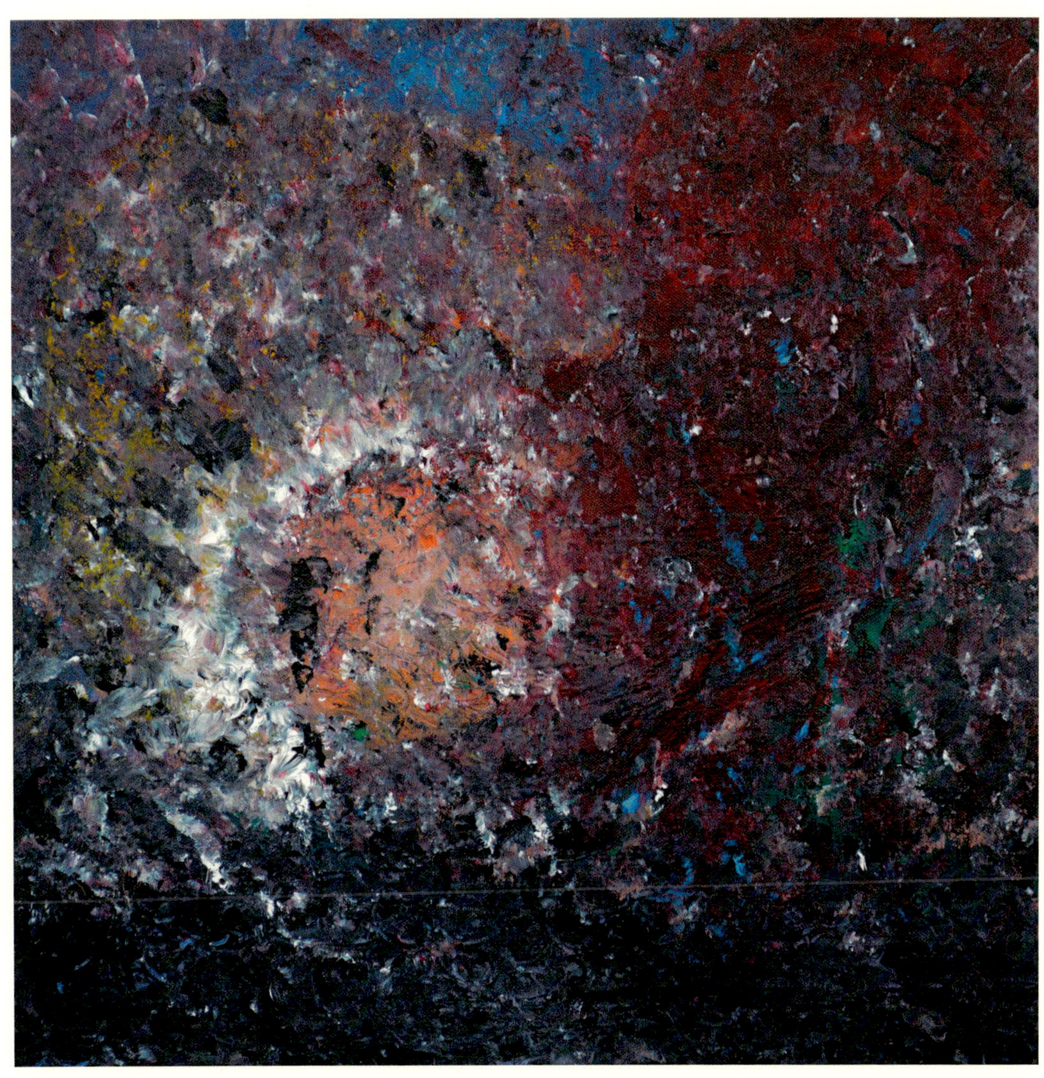

Who knows what will emerge.

Opposite page: 'Rising' PIA acrylic on canvas board, Nicolee

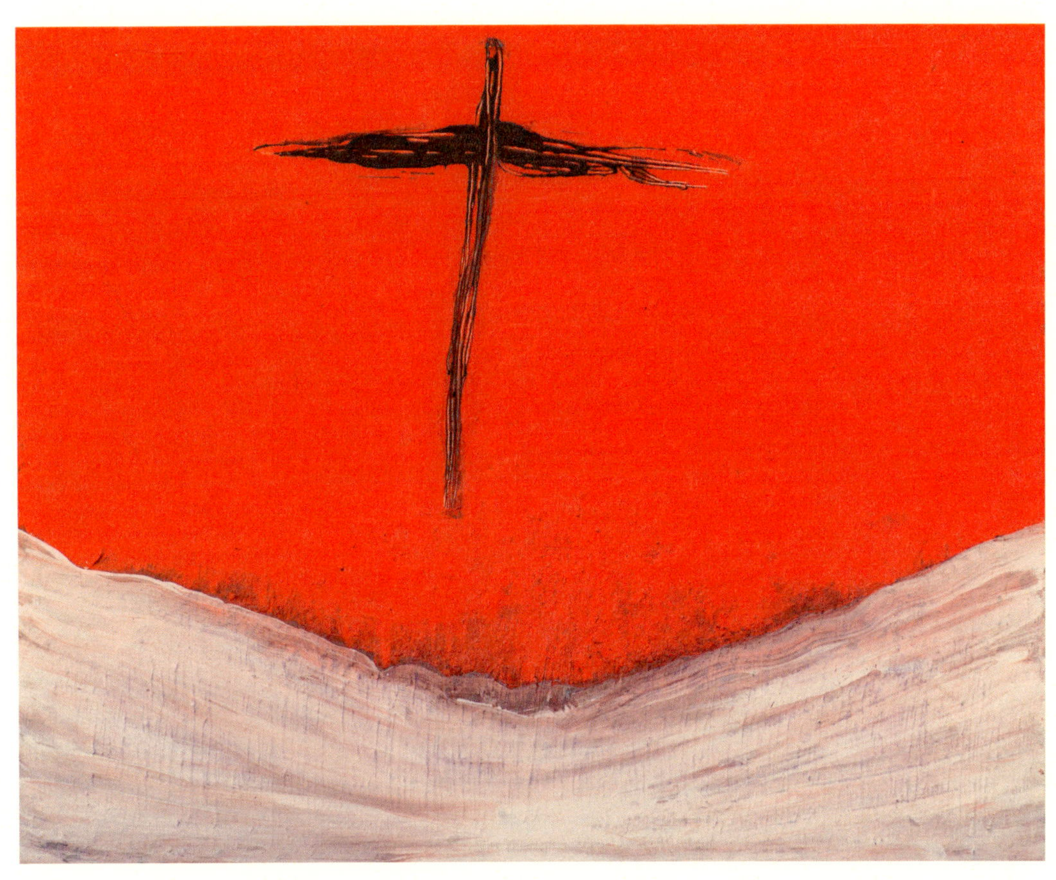

Trust..faith..
awareness..opening..
not knowing
bearing witness
to the cacophony
of Now.

Opposite page: 'Mandala' PIA acrylic on canvas, Nicolee

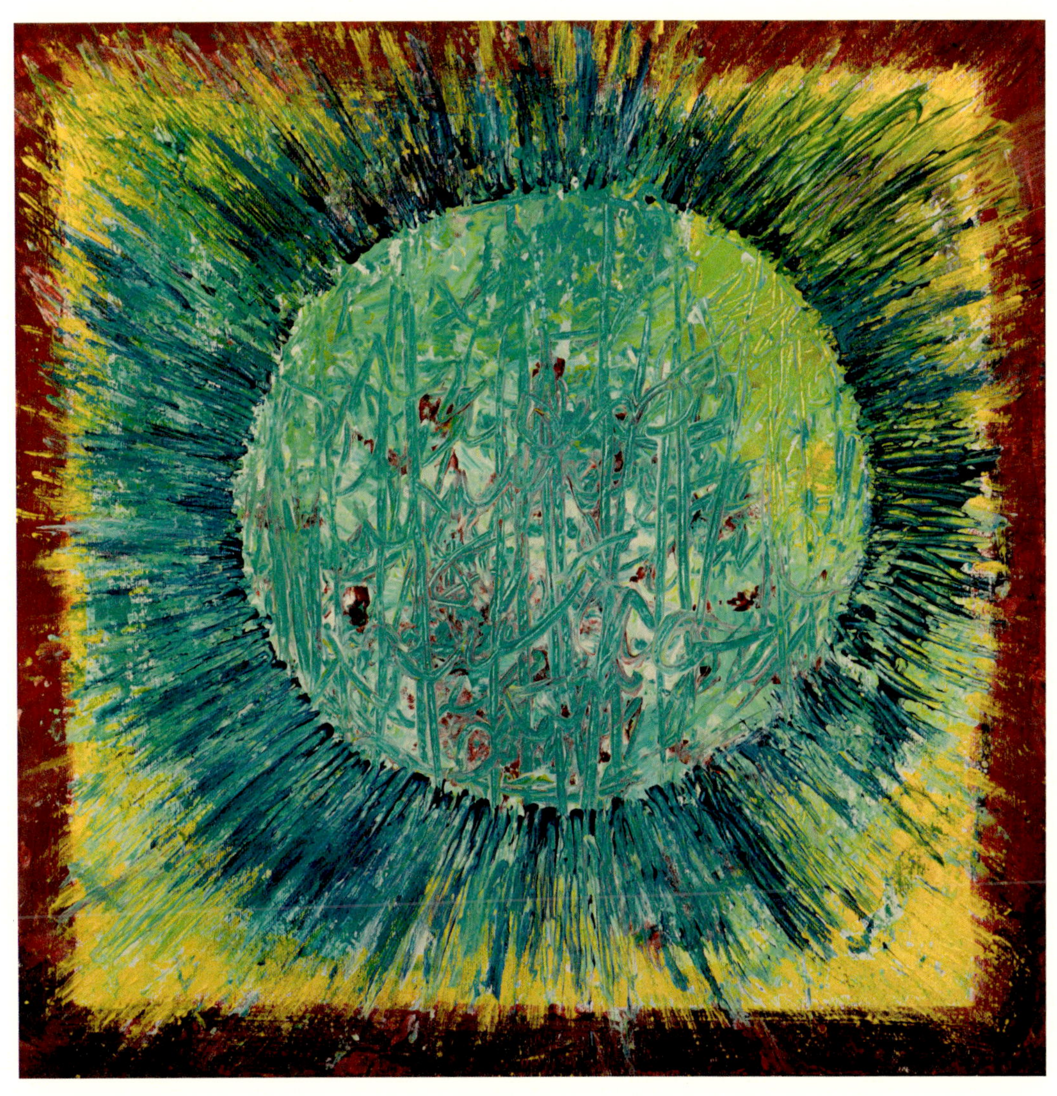

An ephemeral moment,
never to be repeated.....
eternal.

Opposite page: 'Genie' PIA acrylic on canvas, Nicolee

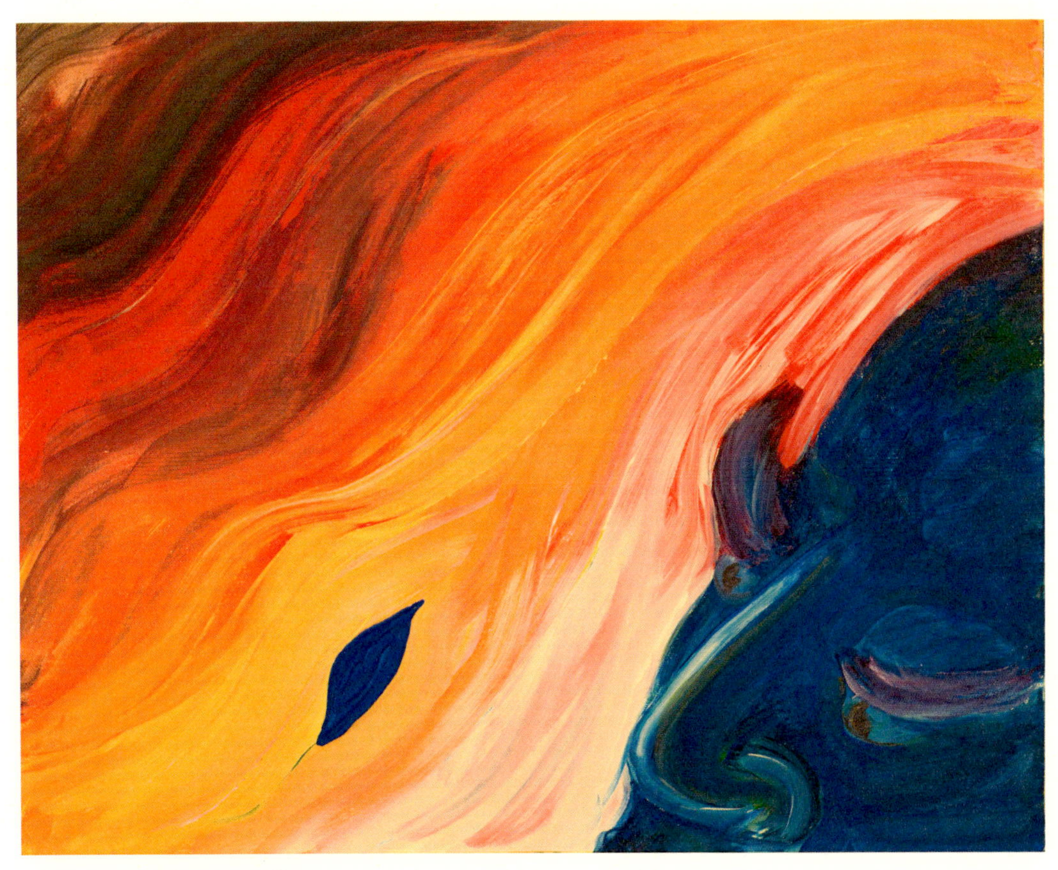

I'm the immediacy
of experience flowing
through creative forms.

Opposite page: 'Tears' PIA acrylic on canvas, Nicolee

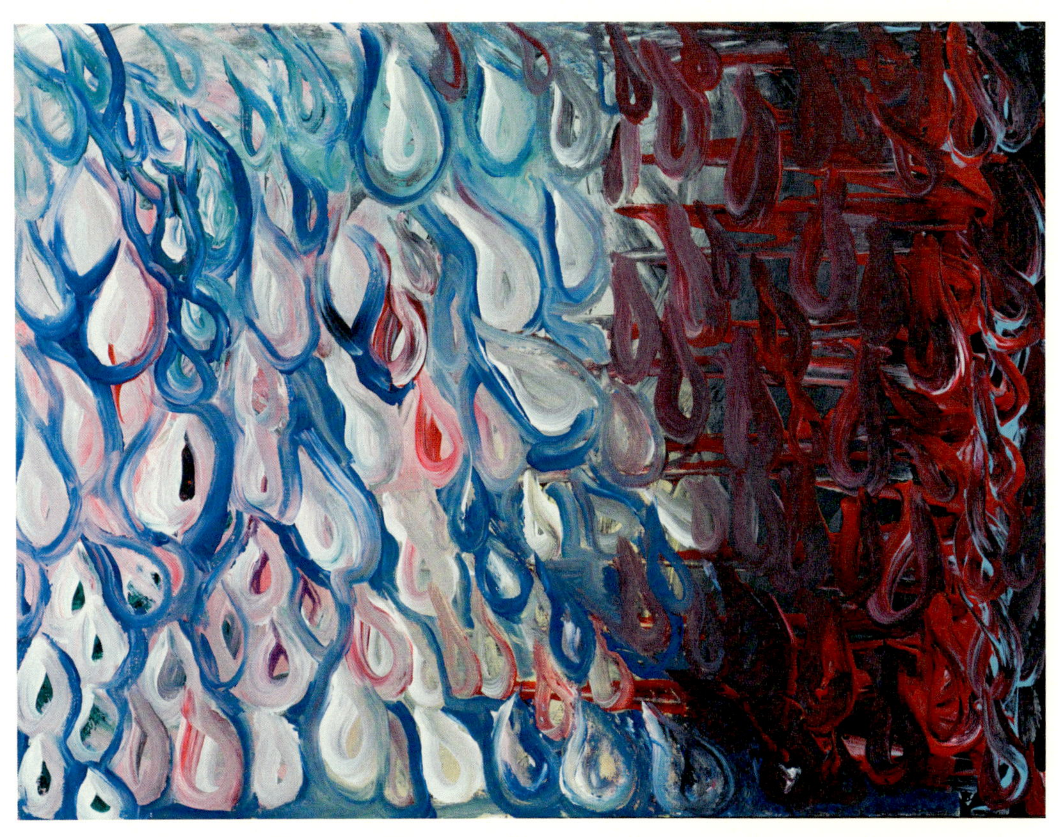

I'm awareness,
I shift between sensations,
emotion, airplanes, laughter,
perception, refrigerator,
motor, clocks
—judgment, confusion,
toilet flushing,
flowing........

Opposite page: 'Mask' PIA acrylic on canvas, Nicolee

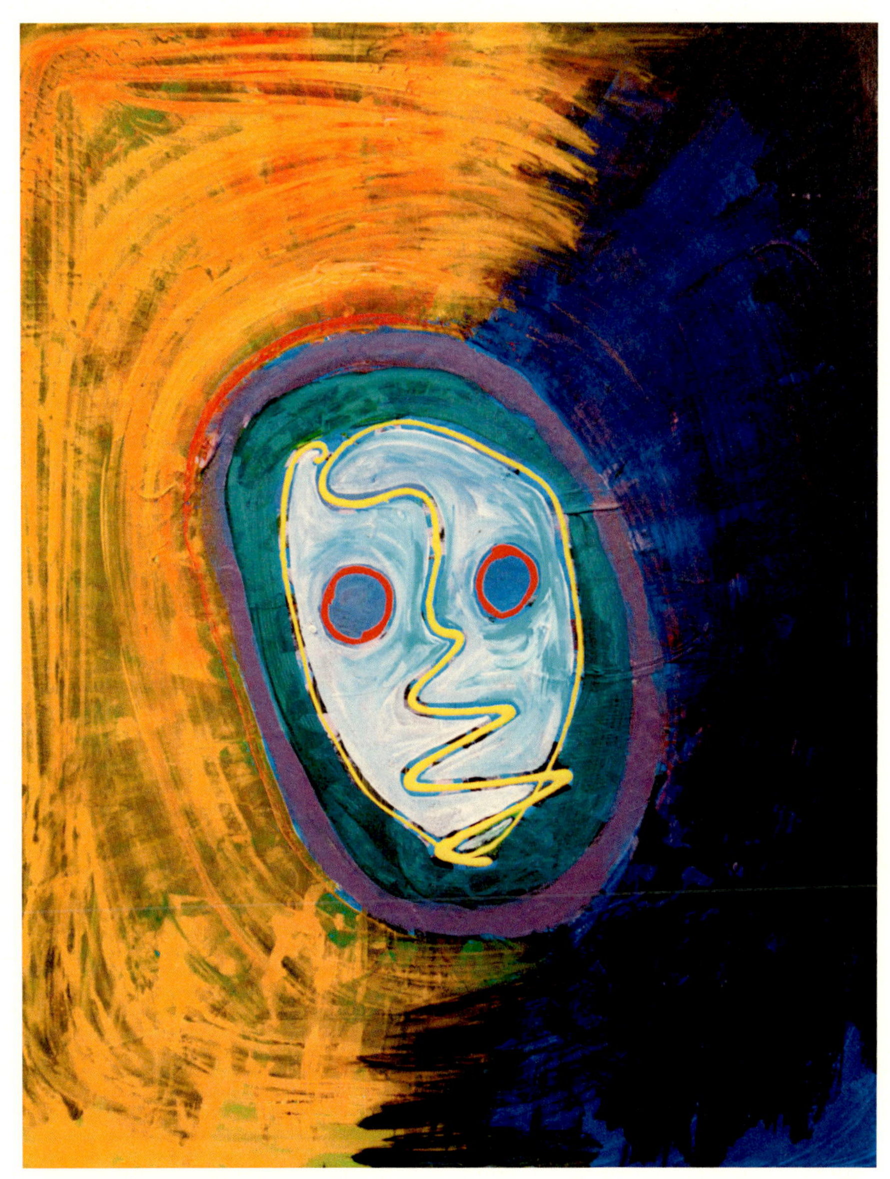

sometimes
moving fast,
sometimes slow,
sometimes
not moving at all.
The end......for now

Opposite page: 'Spears' PIA acrylic on canvas board, Nicolee

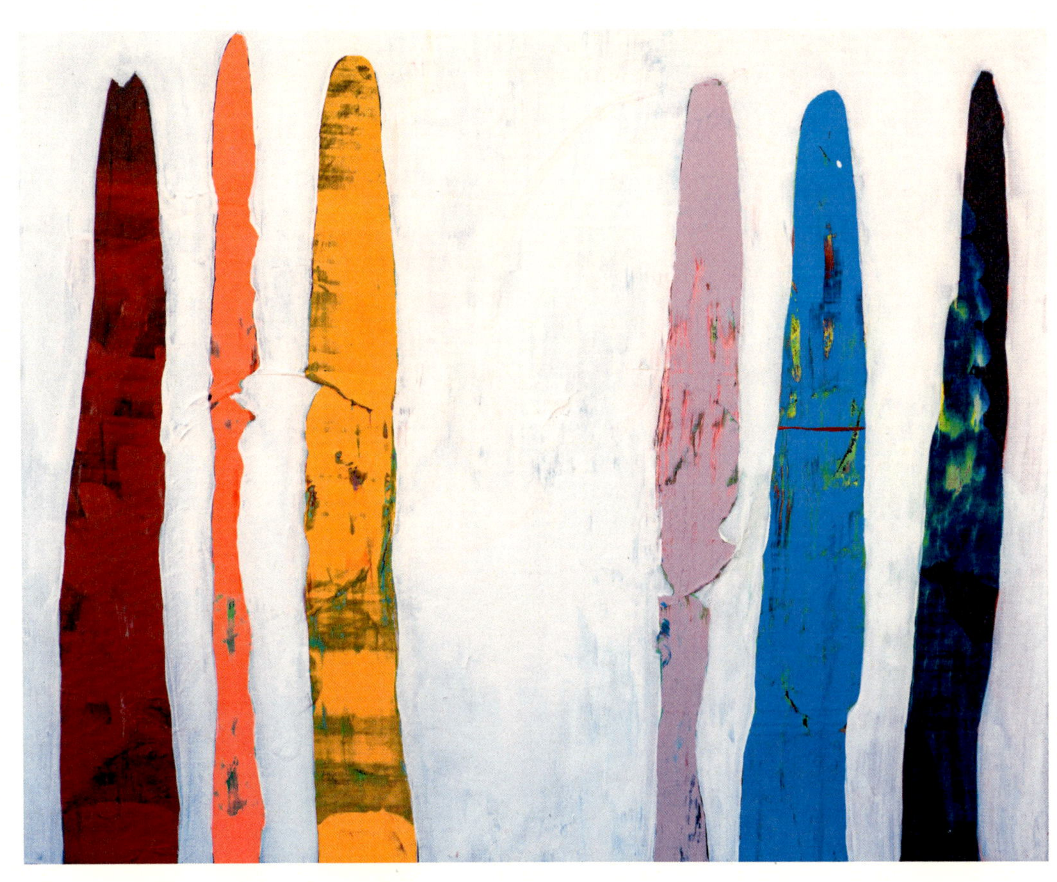

I'm full of possibility,
I can change direction
at any time and am not bound by
antiquated ideas of
how to produce art.

Opposite page: 'Eyes All Over' PIA wood, paint, plastic eyes, Annie Pirruccello

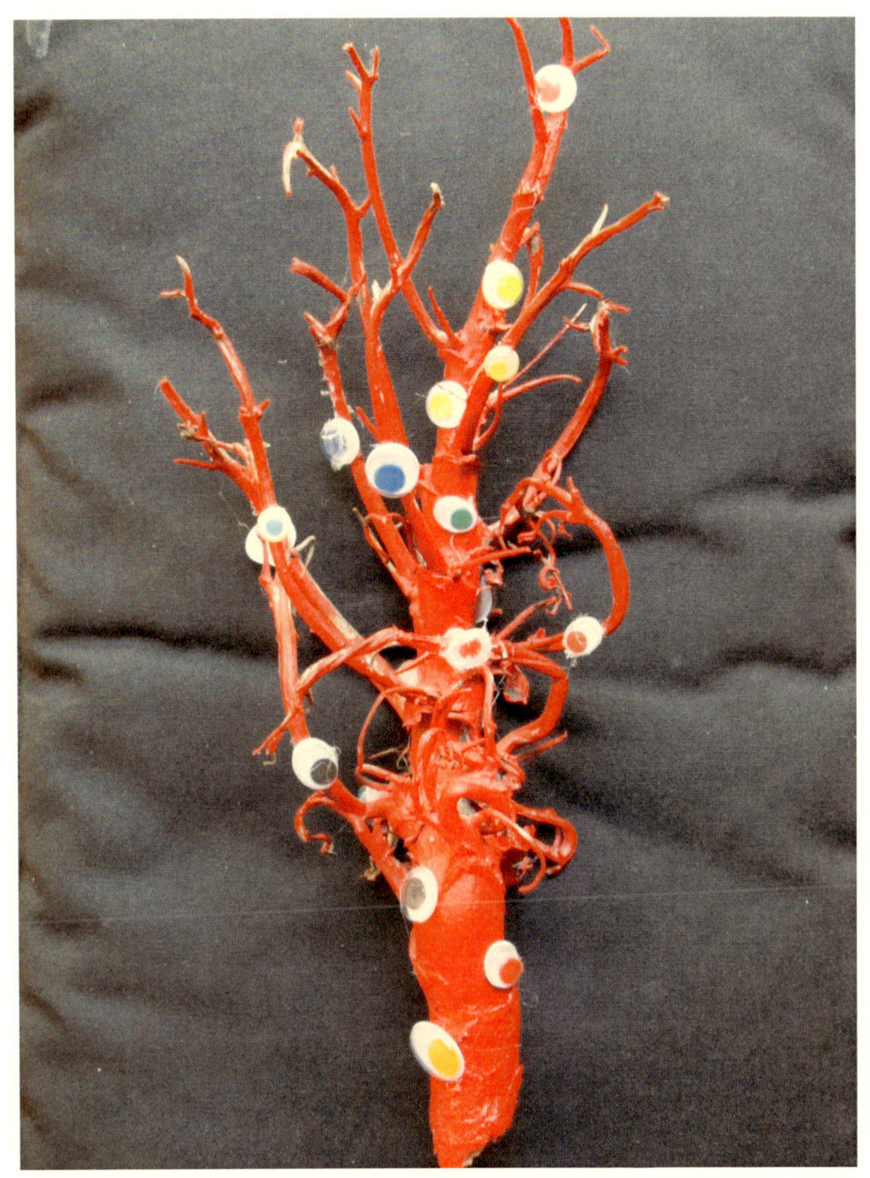

I'm awareness practice that's alive, vital, active.
I'm not limited by being stiff.
I like to engage with all that 'is' in my environment.
I'm fun, playful, scared, dark, depressed
—moods go up and down.

Opposite page: 'Alien Communication' PIA acrylic on canvas, Nicolee

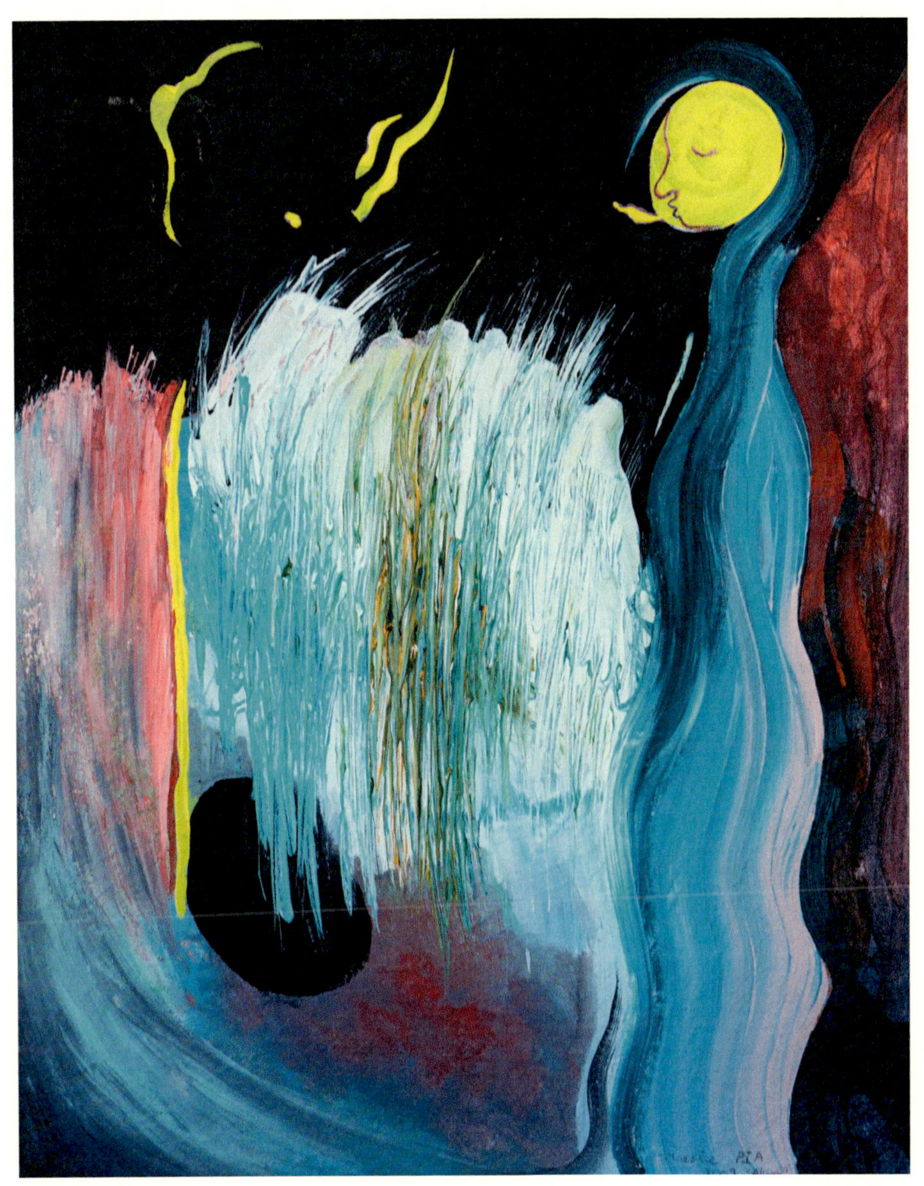

I'm the earth and her creatures
and their creations,
making sounds
grrrrr, bzzzzz, shhmr
I move like wind
and follow what
captures my attention

Opposite page: 'Journeying' PIA acrylic on canvas, Nicolee

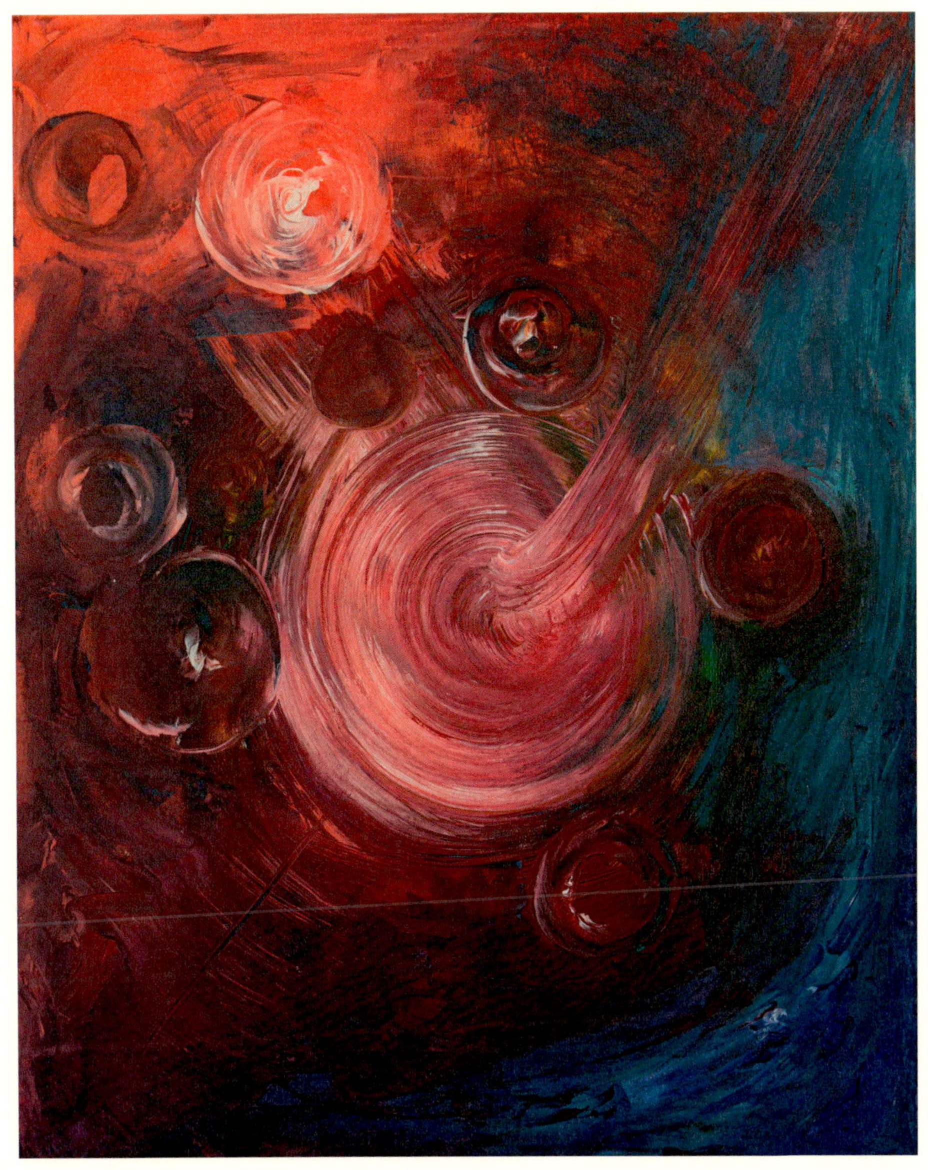

giving shape, form,
color (sometimes)
to the unknown mystery
that emerges in each fleeting,
infinite moment.

Opposite page: 'Swirl' PIA digital art done on computer, Robert Althouse

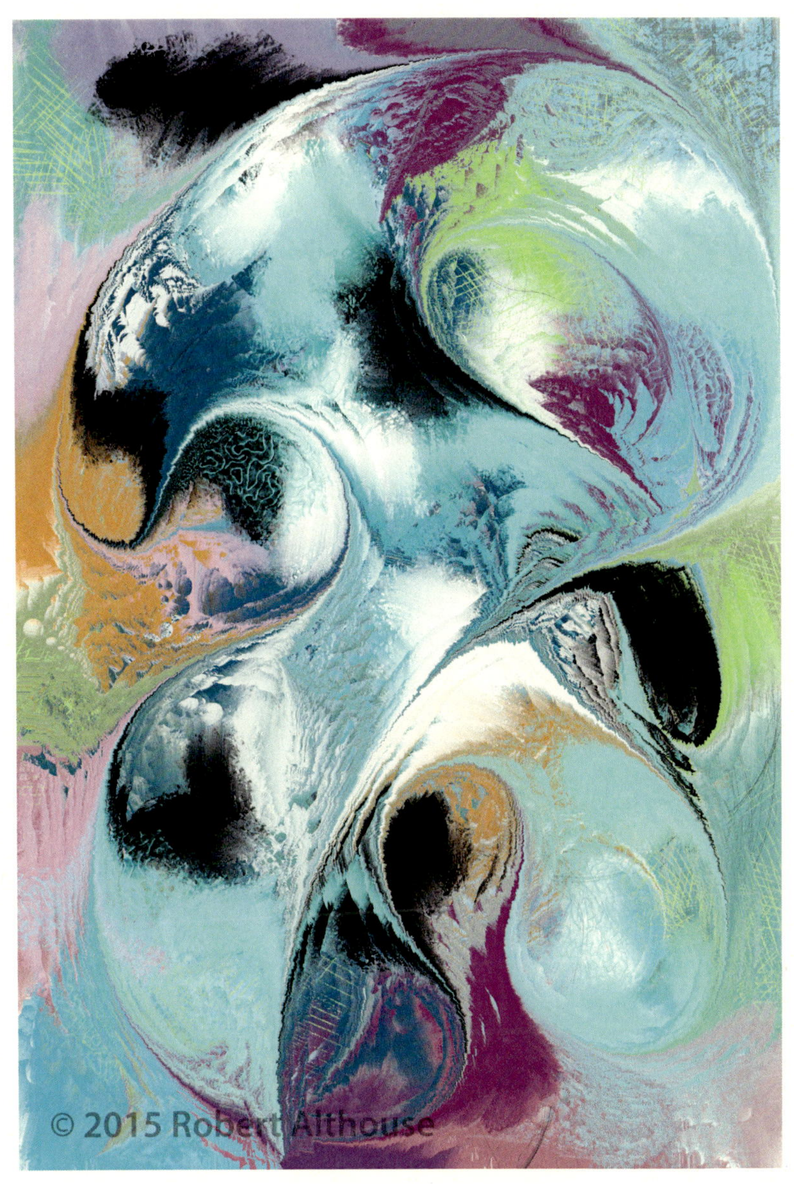
© 2015 Robert Althouse

I'm not held back by fear, flow, outcome
I play in the flowing,
limitless field of Now.

Opposite page: 'Moving' PIA acrylic on canvas, Nicolee

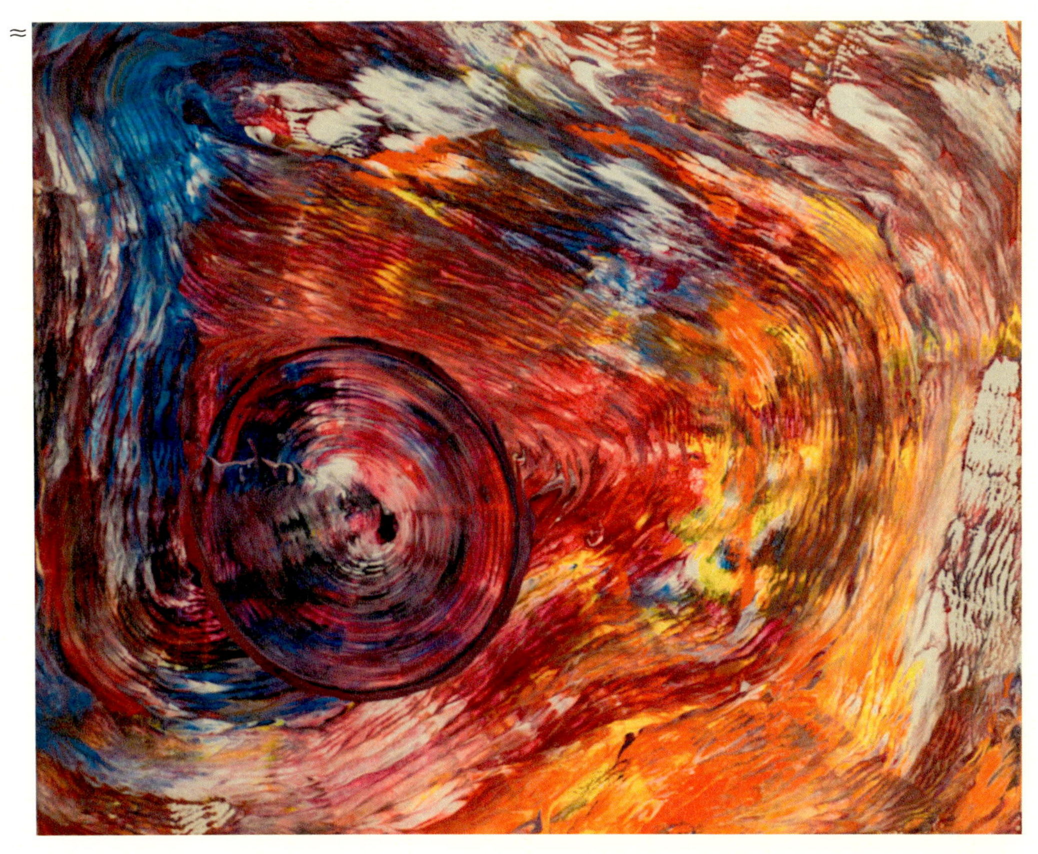

Sometimes
choosing a color
to plop
on the paper / canvas
is where to begin
plop, plop someone
is walking across the floor.
Starting with colors
you're drawn to
squirt some
on a tray

Opposite page: 'Spiral' PIA acrylic on canvas, Nicolee

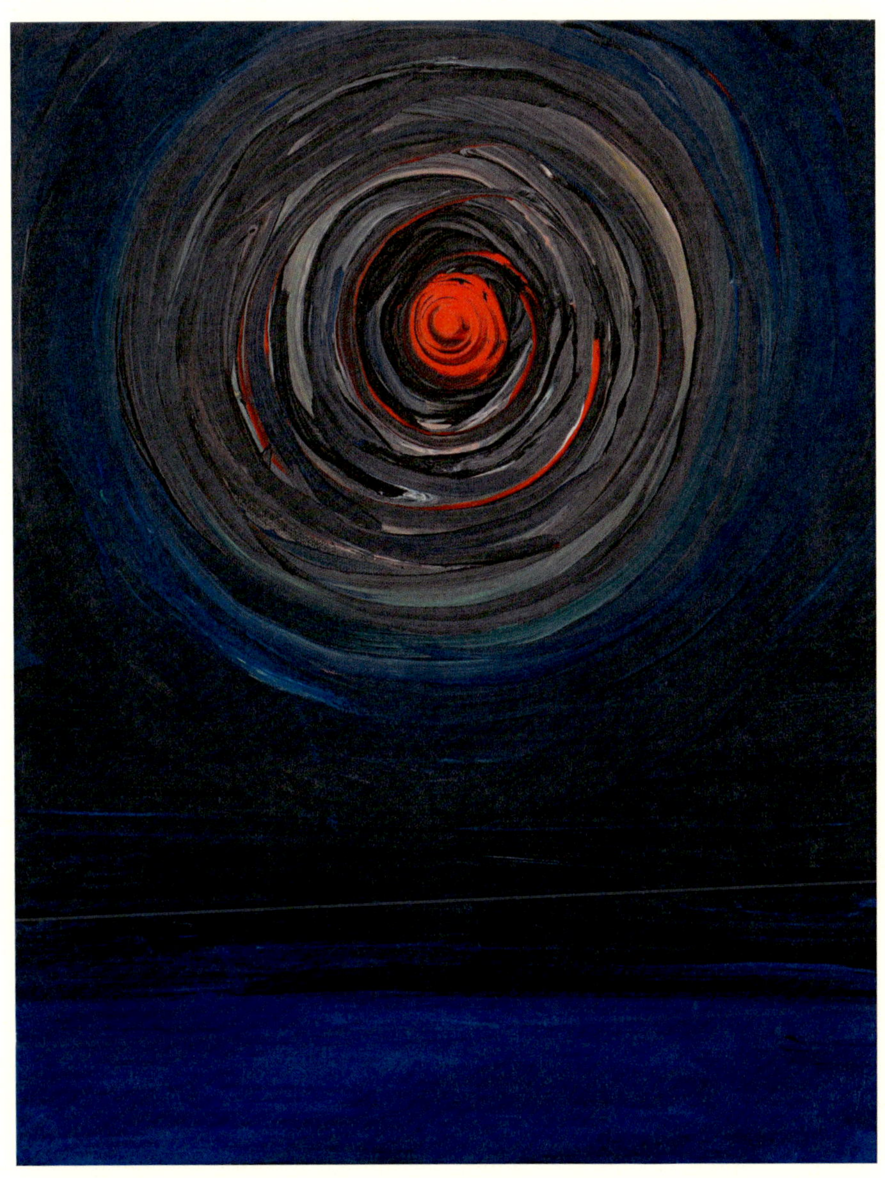

then express the emerging moment
inside or outside makes no difference,
include what unfolds

Opposite page: 'Black Rose' PIA in clay, Joan Hoeberichts

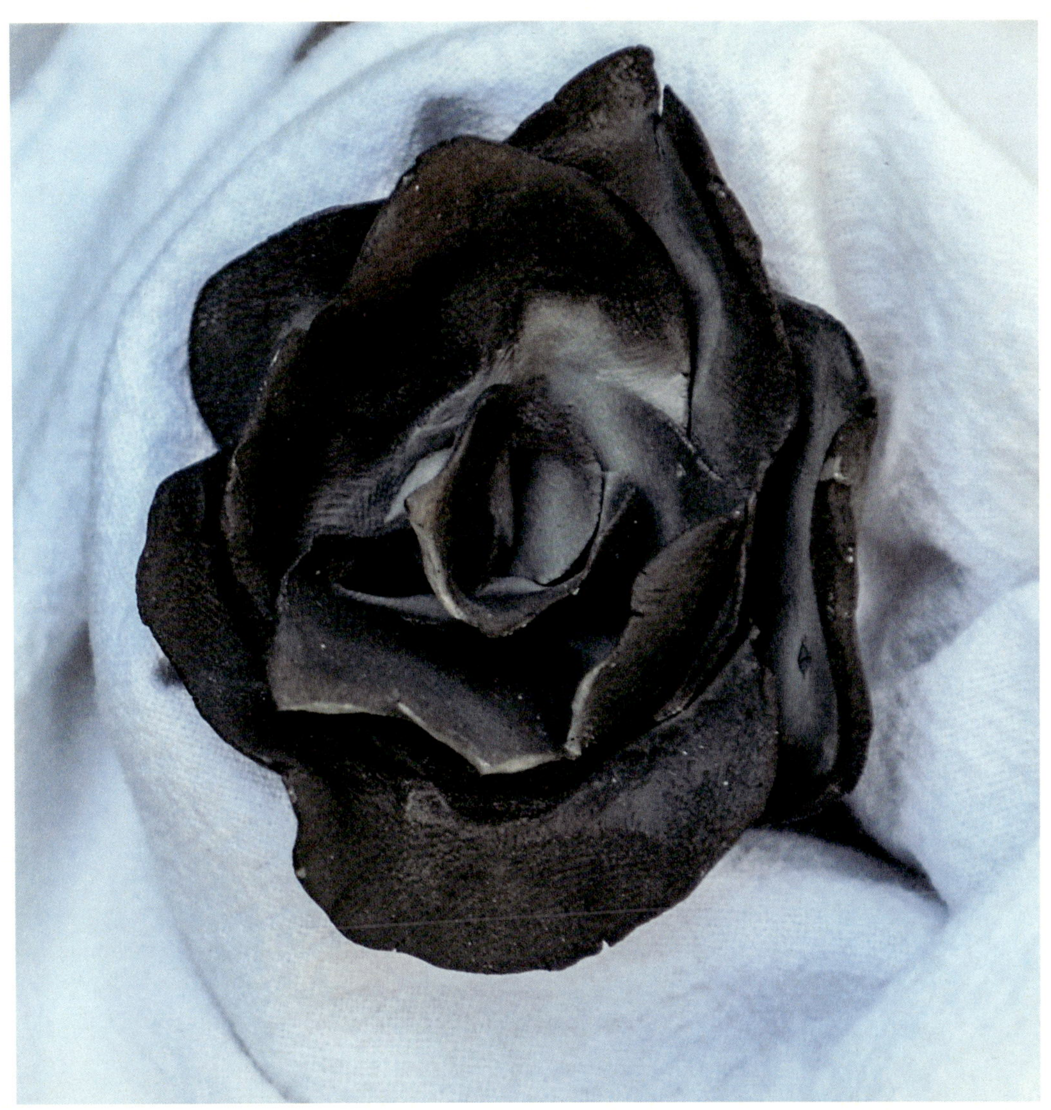

If awareness is speeding along
>>>>>>=======__________^^^^^---------
if awareness is slower and more specific,
that too.
Fear -- what color shape is it?
Include the color/line/shape of
repressing too

Opposite page: 'The Body in Pain' PIA clay, colored wire, hemp, earring wire,
Annie Pirruccello

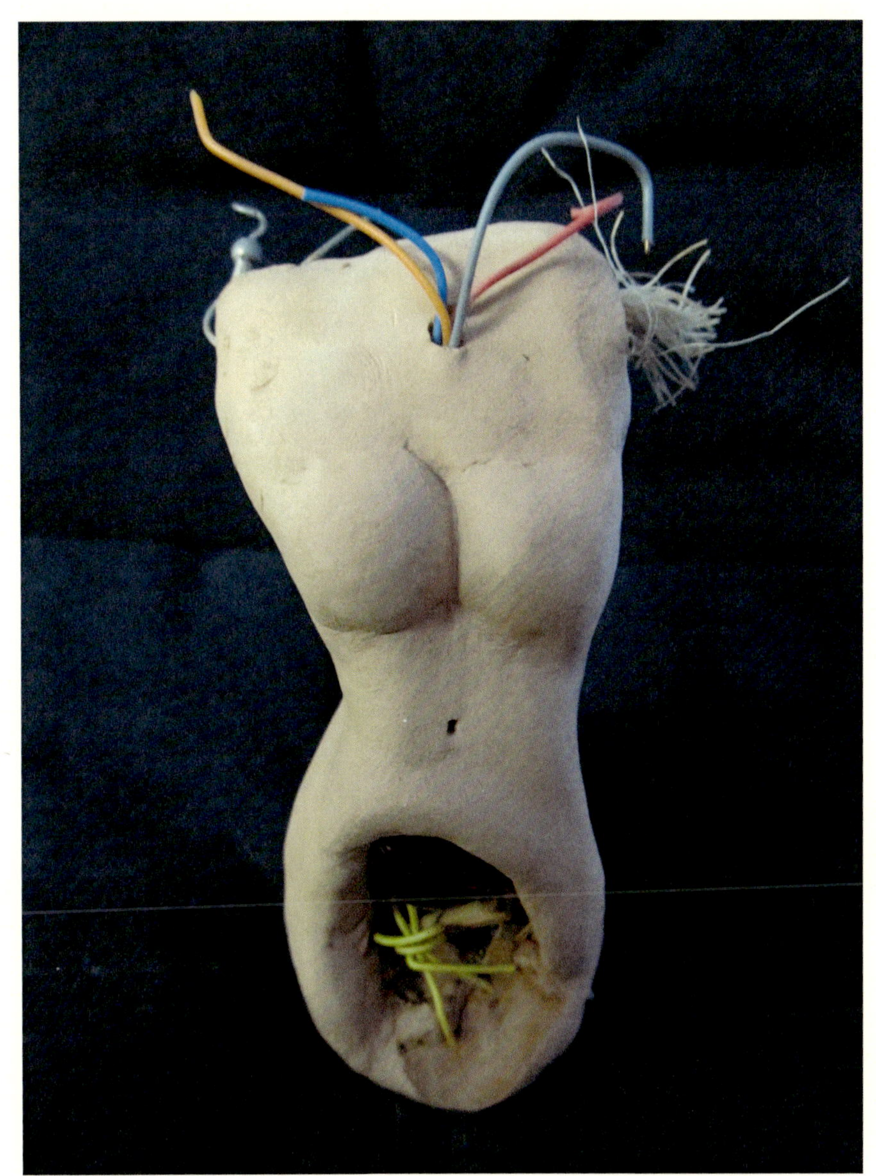

The field of infinity is vast, boundless, boundlessly inclusive.

Opposite page: 'Red Moon' PIA acrylic on canvas, Nicolee

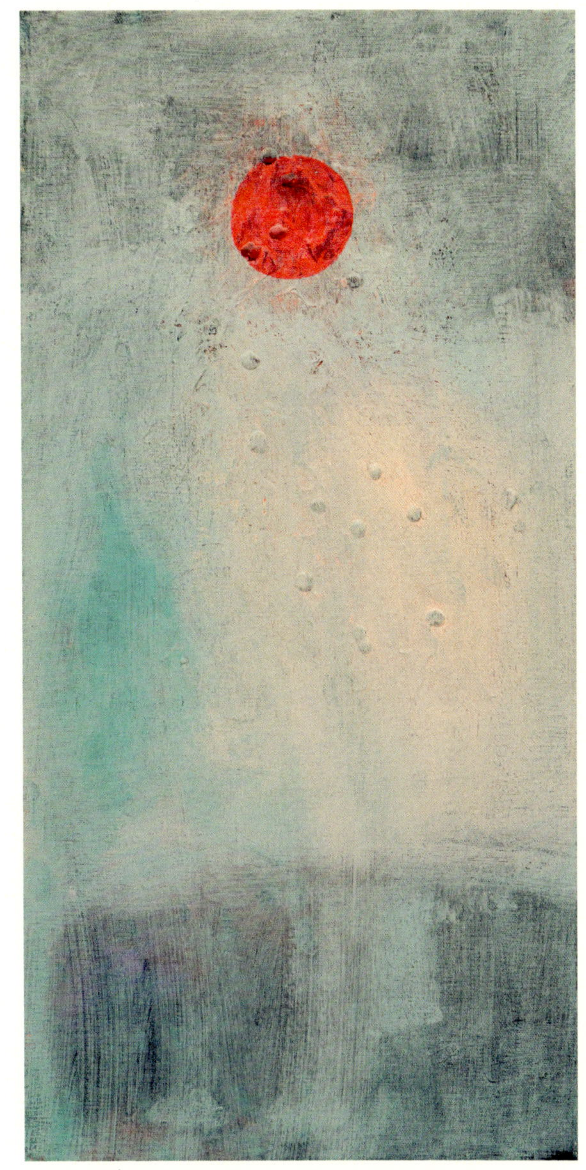

Include whatever 'self' ideas emerge
(self-judgment, opinions, concepts)
scribble them any place and
any size on the canvas/paper.
If you limit yourself, compare, compete
—give color/line/form/sound/movement
to that too.

Opposite page: 'The Critic Can't Keep his Glasses On' PIA acrylic on canvas, Nicolee

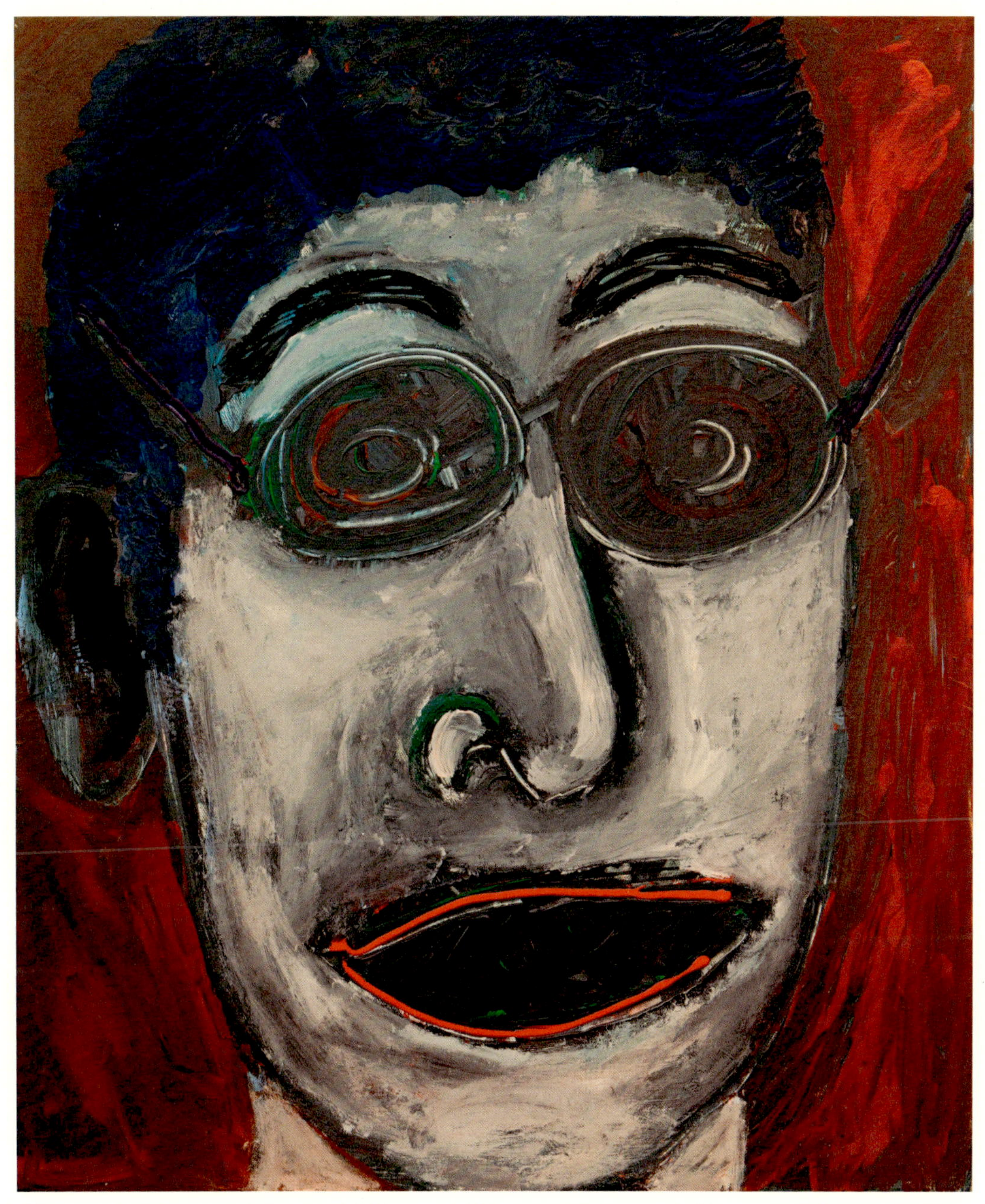

The outcome
is not the piece,
it's you.
You
are teaching yourself
to open wide,
to dance.

Opposite page: 'Woman Dancing' PIA acrylic on canvas, Nicolee

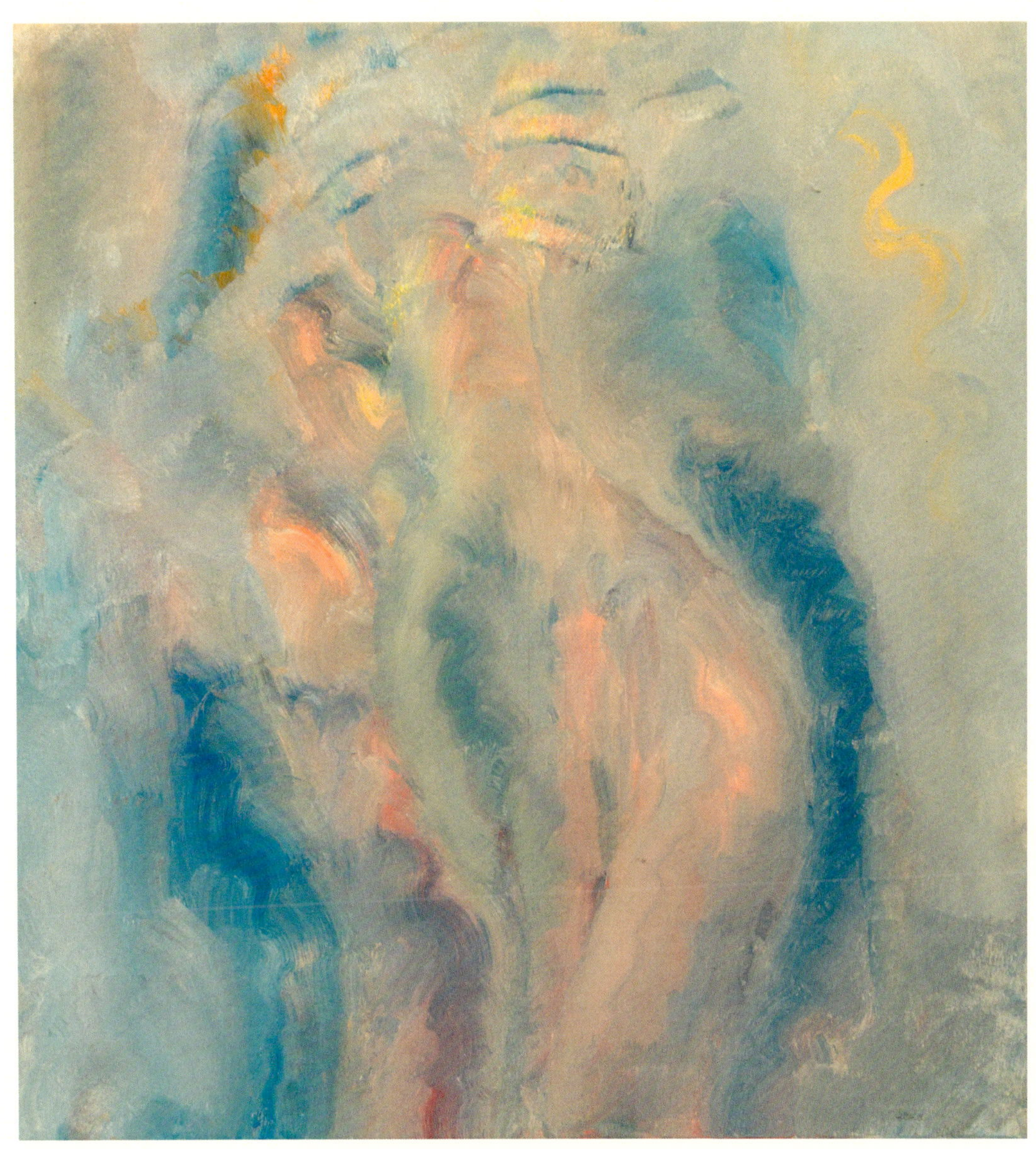

When a creative flow
is present,
follow it……
enjoy.

Opposite page: ‘Flowing’ PIA acrylic on canvas, Nicolee

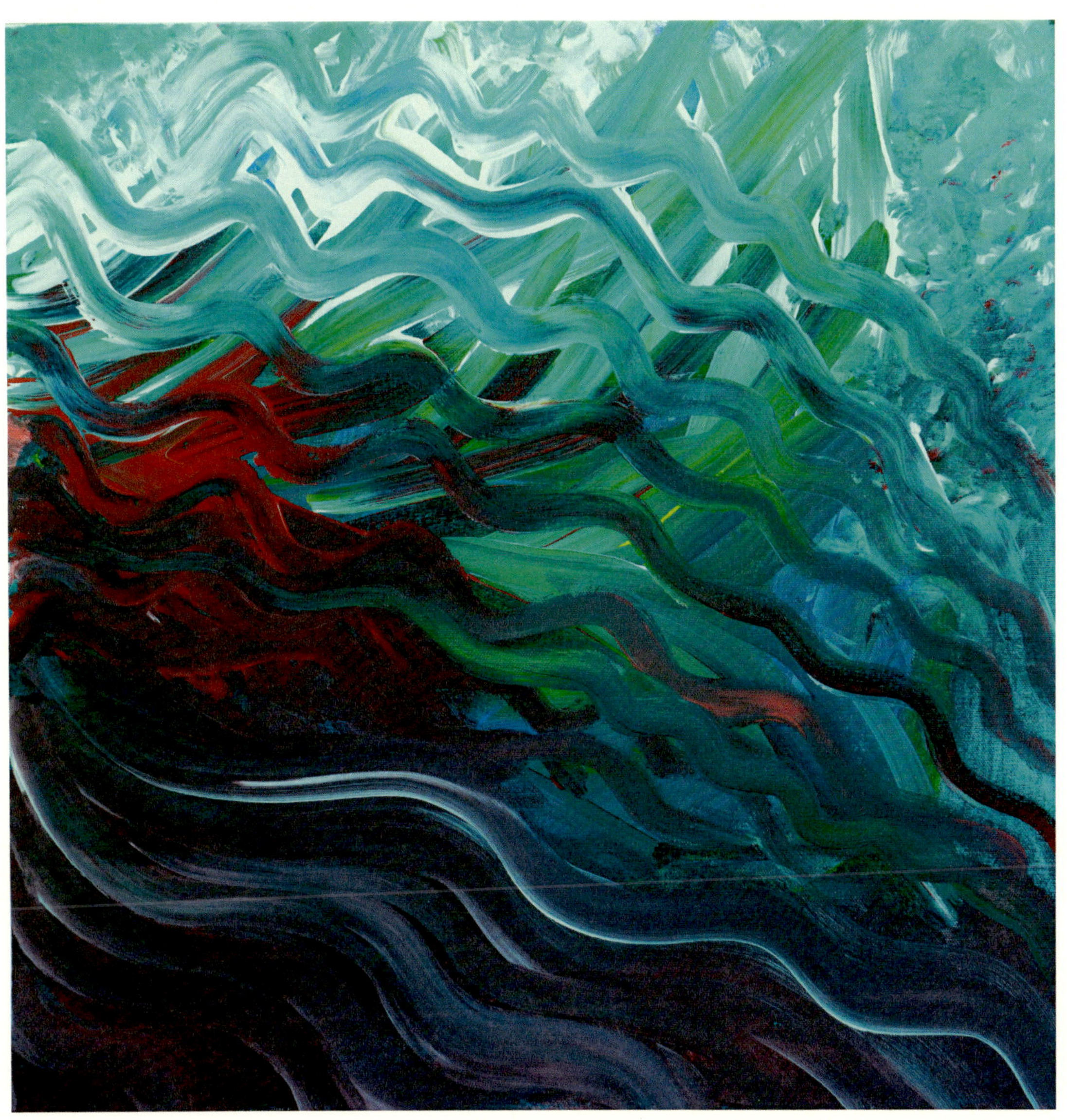

When it's done,
is another surface
ready
to capture the
unfiltered moment?
No matter what media,

Opposite page: 'Abstract' PIA digital art done on computer, Robert Althouse

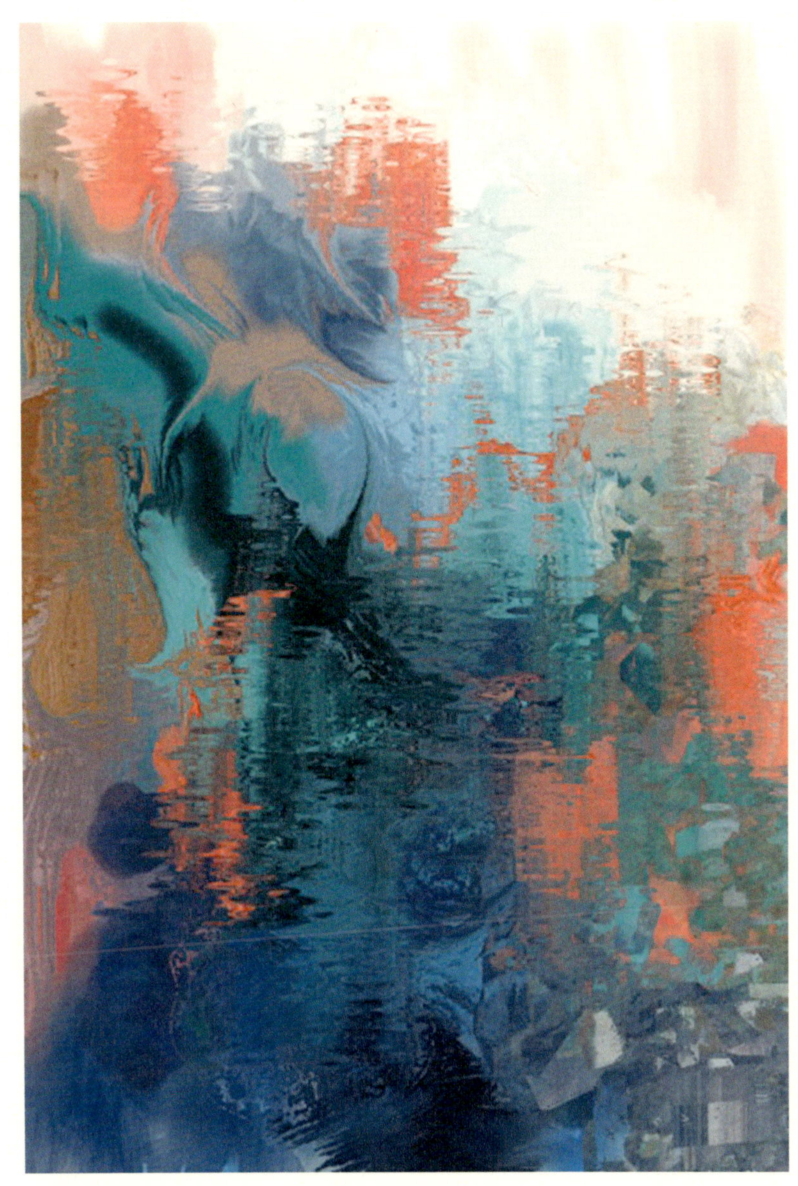

these are
snapshots
of Now.

Opposite page: 'Chinese Lantern' PIA arcylic on canvas, Nicolee

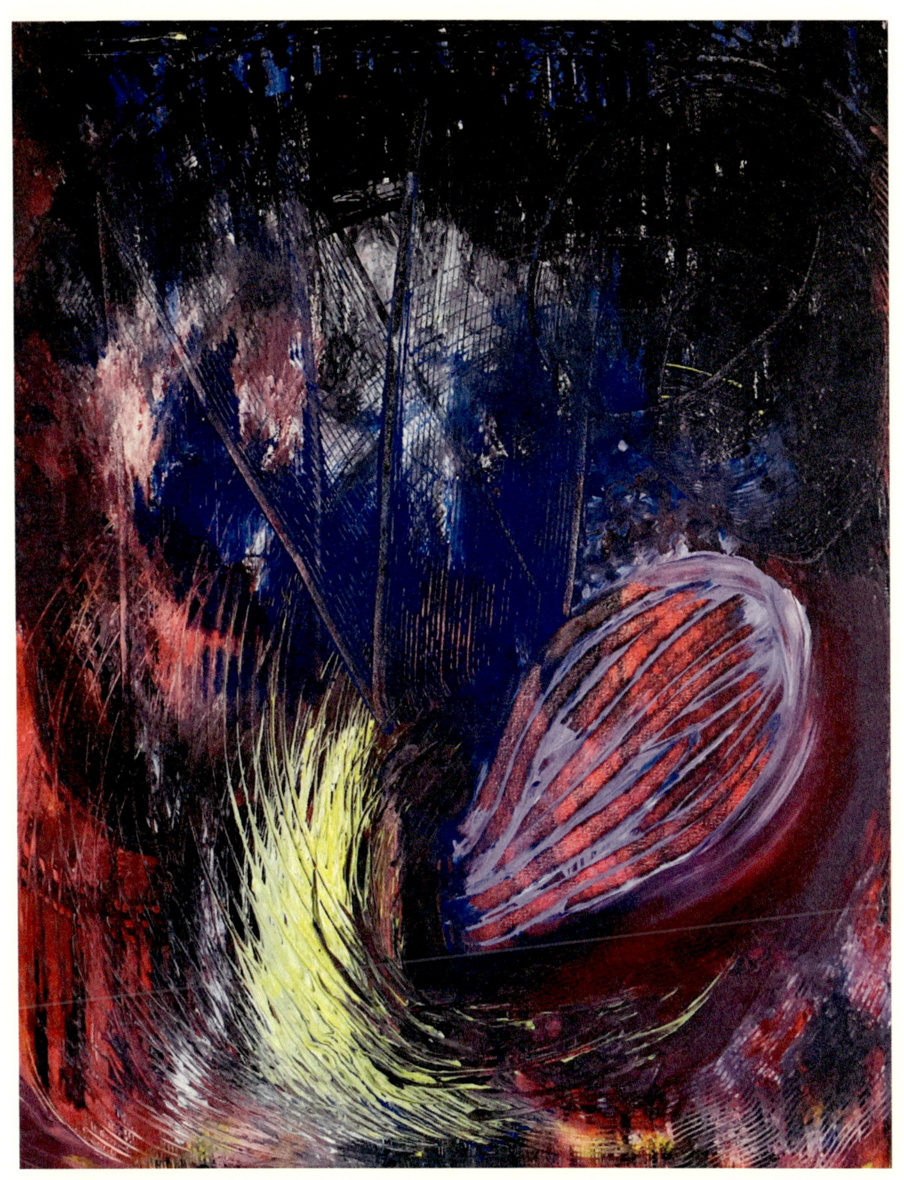

Part Three:

How to Do Practice of Immediacy in the Arts

DIRECTIONS

Take time to sit quietly, breathe, watch your thoughts go by like waves on the ocean or clouds in the sky, notice your body sensations, listen to the sounds... and when you're ready, follow the directions below.

SELECT CREATIVE MEDIUM AND MATERIALS YOU WANT TO WORK WITH

Choose a medium such as art (e.g., pastels, colored pencils, painting, drawing, collage, sculpting), musical instrument, voice, writing, crafts (e.g., beading, wood construction, fabric), or dance/movement, etc.

OPEN TO NOT KNOWING

Come from an attitude of openness, not planning your project or attemping to know in advance what it will look like. Be like an open sky that does not try to control or understand what is passing through.

INCLUDE AND EXPRESS WHAT YOU ARE AWARE OF AS IT SHOWS UP

Use your materials to express whatever finds its way into your awareness, no matter the source. This could include the smell of food cooking, thoughts, the sound of birds chirping, cars going by, memories, body sensations from the hardness of the chair, emotions, sunlight, a taste in the mouth.....It doesn't matter..Include everything!

EXPRESS EXPECTATIONS AS THEY ARE OCCURRING

Expectations include ideas about any kind of "spiritual" or "wisdom" attainment, as well as ideas about creating something attractive, original, beautiful or deep. Expectations become part of the flow of occurrences that you are expressing.

If you enter a creative flow, follow its unfolding

At times you may experience being carried along by a creative wave or current that may have a certain energetic feel to it. It may seem as if you are being lifted up and carried along by a creative flow that directs you towards certain media, forms, textures, and colors. The result of this flow may be an expression that is unified or fragmented, intelligible or unintelligible, familiar or remote. In any case, what you have created is not pre-planned but rather *not knowing* in action.

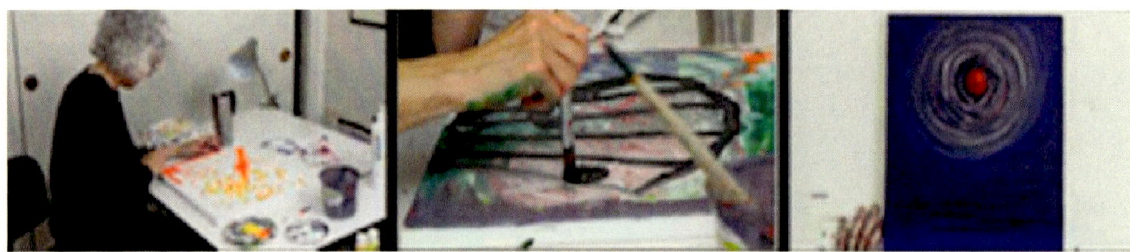

Sample Session

Each session of PIA begins with the selection of some art media, writing, music or movement. So let's suppose you have decided to work with oil pastels and paper for your initial session. After finding a comfortable place to work, choose paper and oil pastel crayons to express what is happening right now:

> Perhaps you are aware of the hardness of the seat of your chair, select a pastel color and give shape to the experience any place on the paper—maybe it's a thick straight line

use another pastel or the same one for the sound of a car going by, perhaps expressed as a squiggly line or the word *swish* expressed anywhere on the paper

the smell of food cooking—what color oil pastel and what shape, and what texture is the smell of food, express it anywhere on the paper

or the feeling of confusion about the new practice—maybe the feeling is expressed in words that you put any place and any size on the paper, or maybe the feeling of confusion is a new color of oil pastel that turns the feeling of confusion into a shape

Now take your oil pastel and express on paper the color, shape and texture of what you are aware of. This may take the form of a simple line, drawing, a word or a splash of color—it makes no difference. Suppose, you are immediately aware of the whizzing of a hummingbird. Again, choose a color and express that sound. *Practice of Immediacy in the Arts* is not about performance—producing a beautiful, original or interesting expression of the hummingbird; it is about using the oil pastel to give color, shape, form or texture to what is present. If 'performing' emerges, give color, shape or words to that anywhere on the paper as well. Perhaps you again hear a hummingbird, and after expressing its sound, you notice a judgment arise about your work: "This is really terrible; I'm no good at this." Once again, express that judgment with your pastels and/or write it any size or place you are drawn to on your paper. The process continues in this way until your session ends; whatever is present—birds, food cooking, whispering voices, a feeling of sadness, a cool breeze, a fantasy about a new job—gets expressed. *No matter what type of art media (water color, acrylics, colored pens, pencil...), writing, music, or movement are used, the process is similar. If a creative flow emerges, follow its unfolding.*

Writing

If you choose writing, open to not knowing, include and express what you are aware of as it shows up, express expectations as they are occurring, if you enter a creative flow follow its unfolding. PIA might look like this: the sound of a car, hardness of the chair, a thought, a feeling, the sound of the clock:

> Rrrrrrrr...........hard....this is stupid!....impatience....tick tock tick tock....

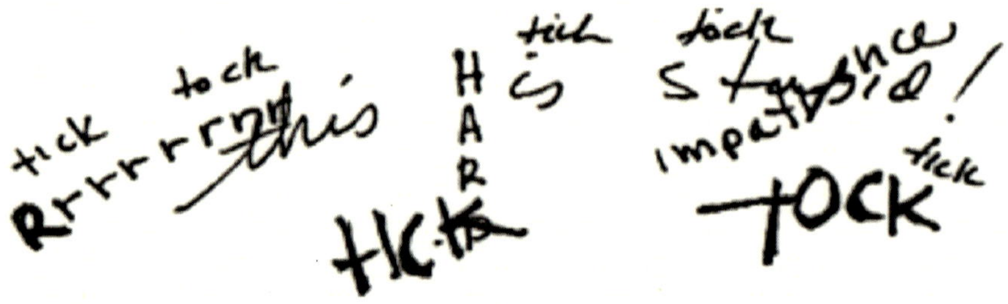

Sometimes what emerges is a poem, a word, a line or just a syllable. Where and how the words are expressed are in accord with your sense of where they belong.

Beads, Wood, other Materials

If you choose beads or want to create a structure of wood and other materials using a glue gun, the same directions apply:

open to not knowing
include and express what you are aware of as it shows up
express expectations as they are occurring
if you enter a creative flow, follow its unfolding

You will need to sit near the materials you'll be using so that they are available. Working with beads, wood and other three dimensional materials is slower than other modalities. Using these media, you may be aware of much more than you are able to express, and that's fine. Just notice whatever is emerging, and continue to attend to your bead work, or structure.

Clay

If you choose clay, follow the general instructions for PIA.

Musical Instruments

If music is the medium you choose, the instructions for PIA are the same as with other media. Play or sing an expression of what is occurring. It may be a scale or riff, a chord or melody, or even unmusical sounds. You may use rhythm, tempo, dynamics and all the elements of music to express the immediate moment.

Mixing Modalities

Please feel free to work with several modalities at the same time if that's appropriate for you. For example, use art + words, words + clay + movement, or music + movement or any combinations that are appealing to you. The same directions apply.

Resistance

Resistance or repulsion is one of the five hindrances to awareness practice, and it may arise when you are introduced to or engaging with PIA. Sometimes this is due to certain ideas about what creativity should look like. Some people experience fear at the sight of creative media they haven't used since childhood, or it may happen that people feel inhibited because they believe they need to create an acceptable or beautiful finished product.

There is nothing wrong with resistance, and in PIA it is included and expressed in the same way as whatever else is arising in the moment. One of the effects of PIA is learning how to swim in the midst of things—including your judgments and opinions.

Again, please take a look at www.practiceofimmediacy.com/pia-videos for the three short videos. Two of the videos show the practice of PIA in acrylics on canvas, and the third one is PIA using oil pastel on paper. May you enjoy the endless possibilities of this unfolding, creative moment.

Part Four: Revised PIA (PIA+)

Part Four presents examples of my revised PIA (PIA+) using acrylic on canvas, followed by a description of my process. Also included in this section is a revised PIA poem by Vivienne Lund. Whereas pure PIA is unplanned, emerging in the moment, revised PIA starts with PIA and then is worked on at a later time. In revised PIA, one is editing, revising, changing the piece in accord with one's own creative sensibility.

For professional artists and representational artists, pure PIA can be a creative exercise to open up the doldrums or flat, stuck places that professionals might encounter. Revised PIA could provide a venue for representational artists who might start with PIA and then use their technical training and sensibility to create a representational piece. The same approach could also be used by writers, musicians, and dancers.

The image below is a pure PIA completed in one sitting. I did not like the piece, so I put it away with recycled canvases that I reuse for future PIA sessions. About a year later, I picked up this canvas and saw it completely differently.

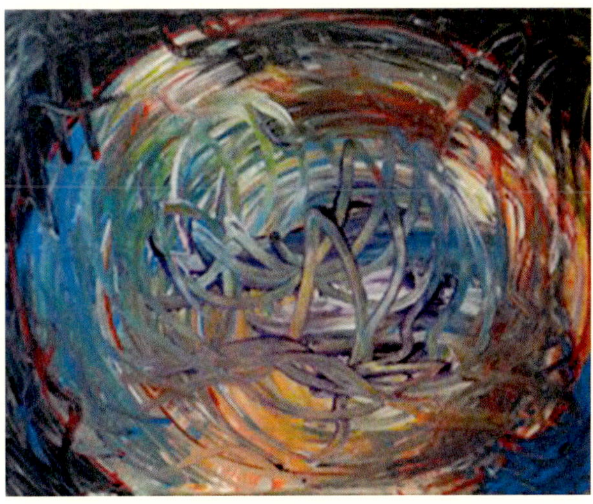

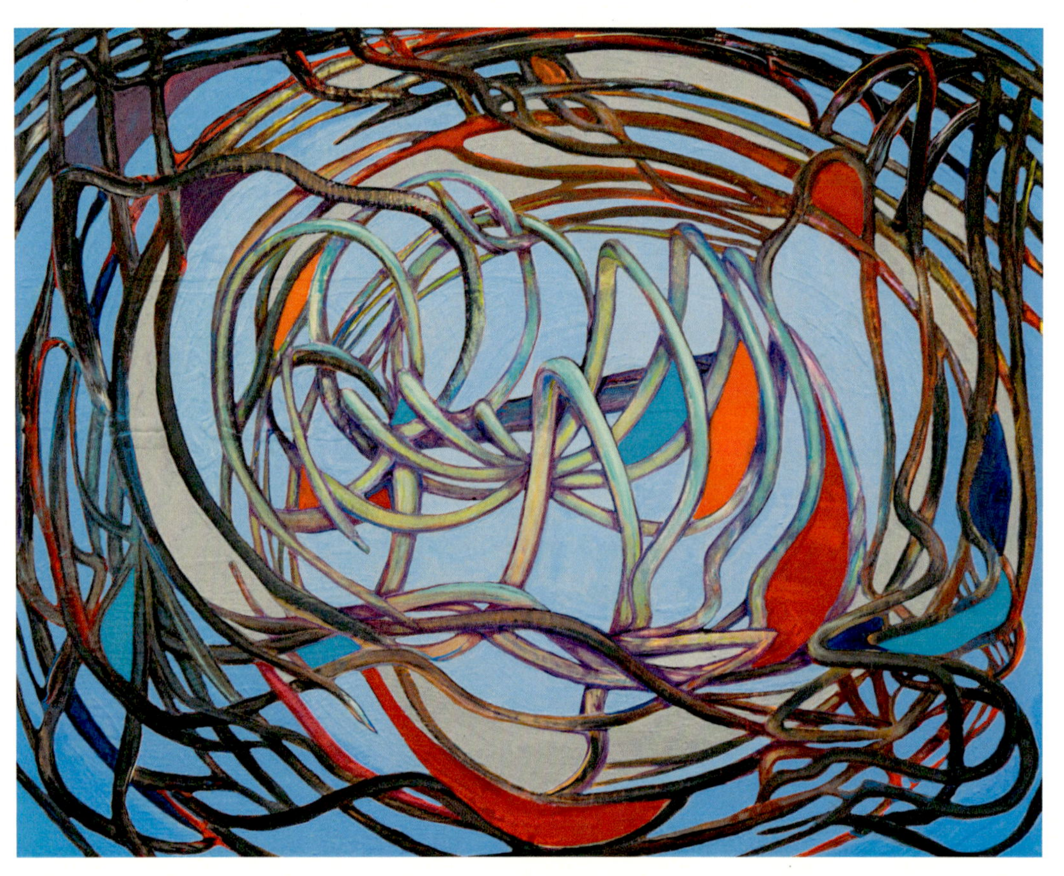

In revising the PIA piece 'Untangling,' I began releasing the flowing lines by painting in the negative spaces with different colors and then saw how graded shades of blue, darker on the outer part of the painting and lighter blue toward the center, really made a difference. That allowed me to see the curving lines in a whole new way—like vines that were untangling and that needed shading and different colors to bring them out more. Whereas PIA is done in one session, I worked on 'Untangling' for months until I felt it was done.

Opposite page: 'Untangling' PIA+ acrylic on canvas, Nicolee

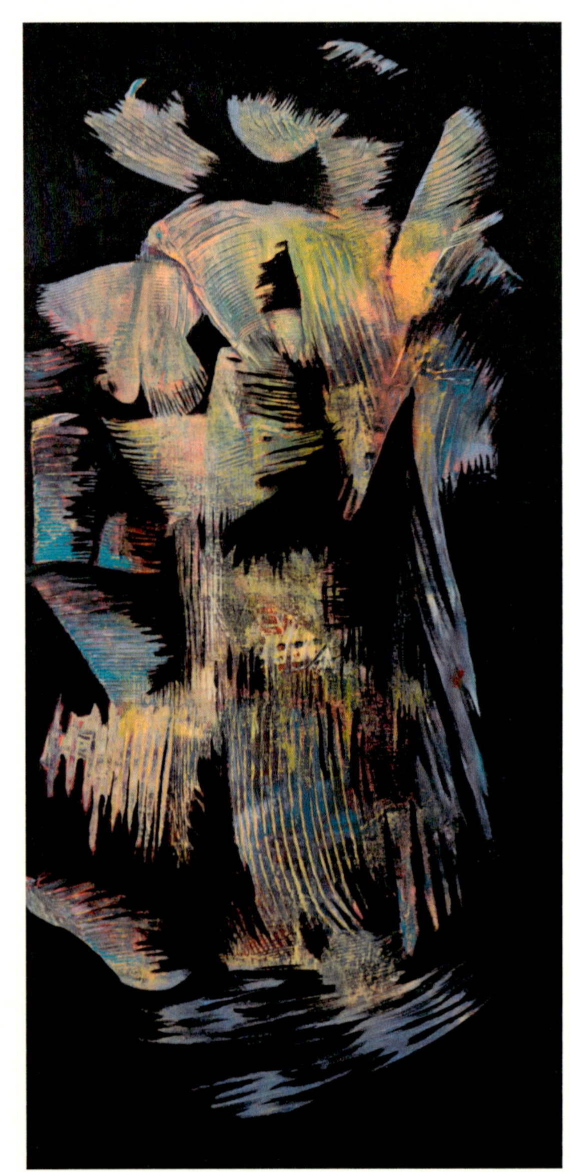

'Shaman's Dream' began as PIA, full of everything emerging in the moment, but not a piece I'd keep. So I began another PIA and at the end used the first canvas to wipe extra paint on while cleaning up the paint brushes. When I looked at the canvas at a later time, all of a sudden, the canvas began to have a life that wanted to be seen. I painted black where I felt it belonged and began to see birds flying and a shaman in the lower part of the canvas. I think I was attuned to seeing this because I had been training with a medicine woman from 2000-2007. 'Shaman's Dream' was completed in 2004, in the middle of my training with her.

Opposite page: 'Shaman's Dream,' PIA+ acrylic on canvas, Nicolee

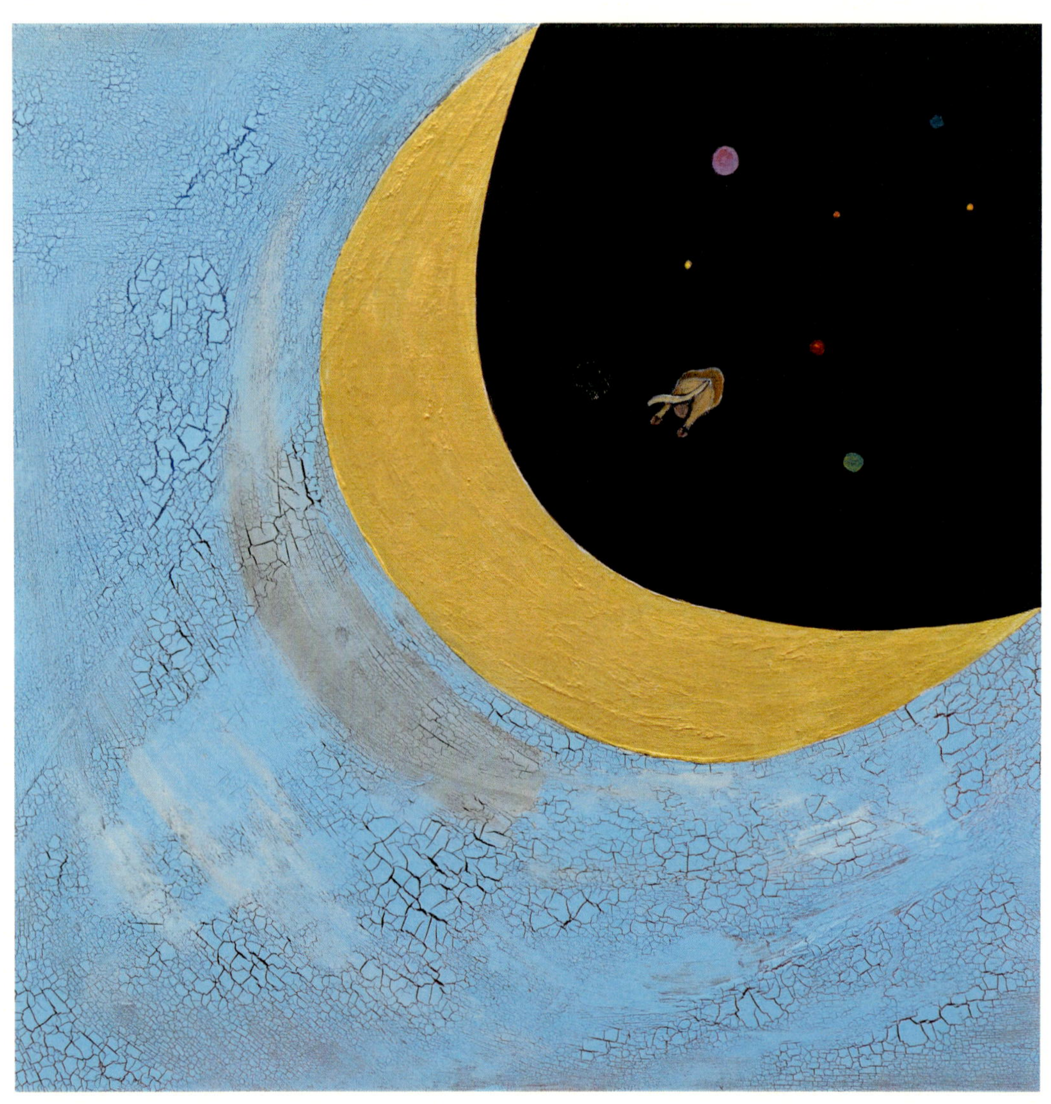

'After the Cow Jumped Over the Moon' began as PIA and was put in the recycle pile for a future PIA session. When I pulled out the canvas, I began doing PIA on top of the acrylic paint of the previous canvas. I needed to stop to go do something else and left the painting for several days. When I returned, the slickness of the previous paint had caused a cracking of the blue paint that was on top of it. In my mind's eye, while looking at the serendipity of what had happened, I began to see a cow jumping over the moon. And that's what I painted.

Opposite page: 'After the Cow Jumped Over the Moon', PIA+ acrylic on canvas, Nicolee

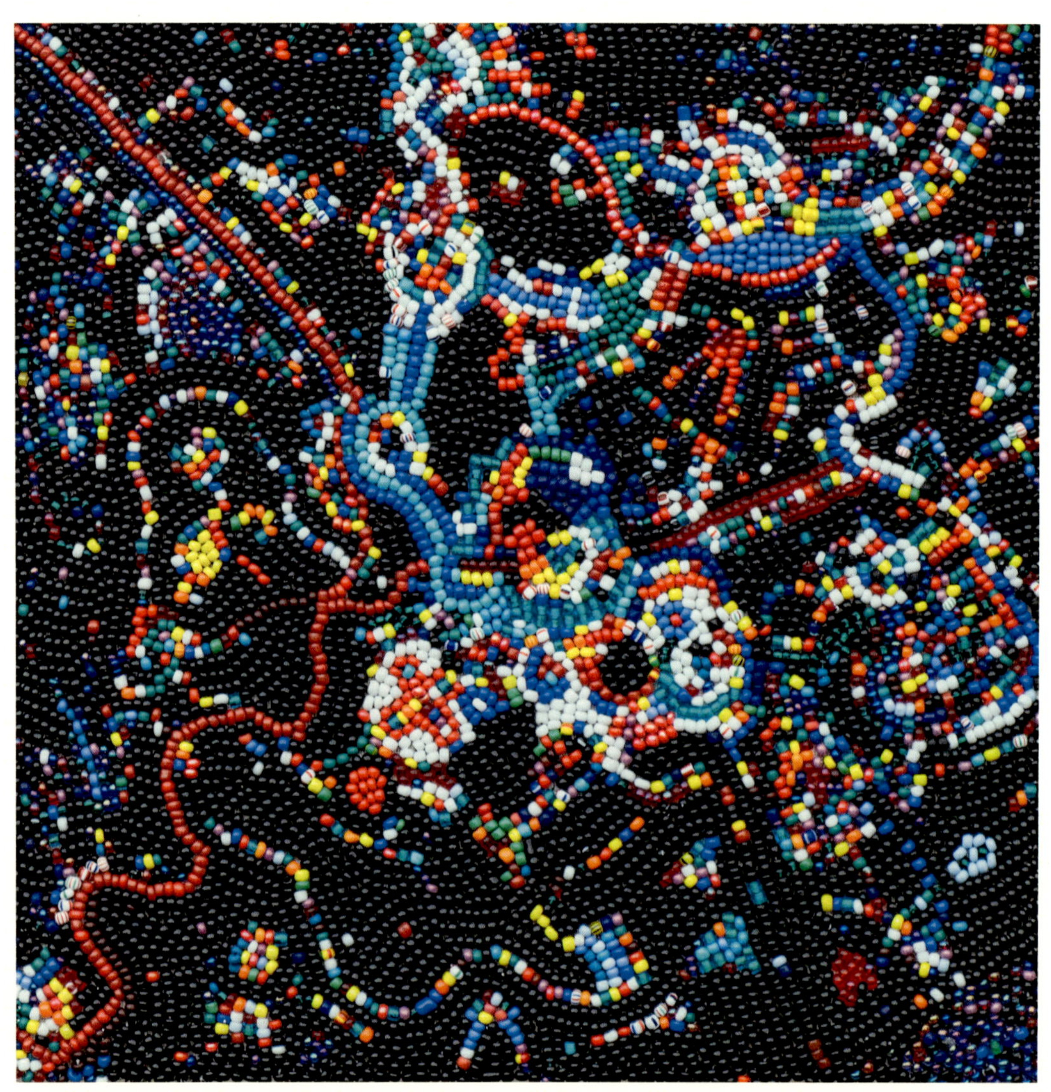

I was inspired by Yoruba beadwork I had seen at an exhibit when I was 25 and decided to capture in beadwork five images that would express my opening process over the course of my life. Each of these beadwork projects are 10x10." I've done one per decade: ages 25-35, 35-45, 45-55. I started the fourth one in 2003 and was curious to try PIA in beadwork to see if it was possible. Each bead was done one at a time following PIA directions (not knowing, include what you are aware of as it shows up, express expectations as they are occurring, if you enter a creative flow, follow its unfolding). When the beadwork was finished, I used black acrylic to paint several white beads black. It's a slow process and took 12 years to complete.

Opposite page: 'Beadwork' PIA+ 10x10" cloth stretched over wood frame, Nicolee

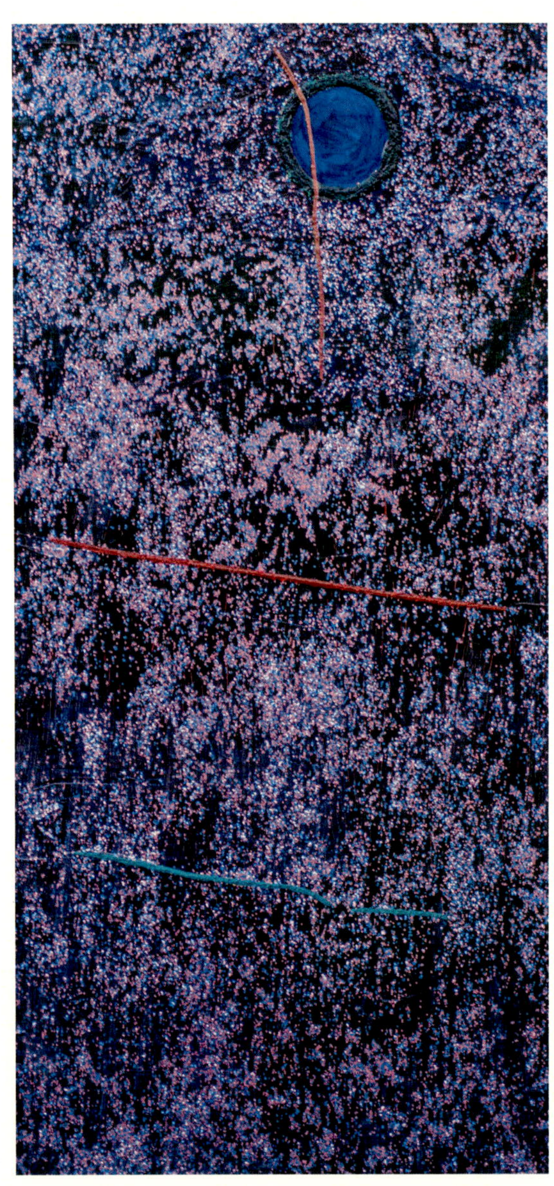

‘Birth, Living, Letting Go’ began as PIA painted on a long, thin piece of plexiglass. I put the PIA piece aside at the end of the session for recycling. Several months later I looked at it again and could see a circle in the old PIA, and so I painted the circle, then lines that meant to me, birth, living and letting go (the green line for letting go is broken and is easier to see in person). I painted the background in varying shades of red, then dark blue, then I had an *antojo*—I lived in Mexico as a child, and have always found the word *antojo* to be much richer than an ‘urge.’ My *antojo* was to add sparkles, but I needed to figure out how to do that so they would stick. I ordered sparkles on the web as well as a shiny gel medium that would hold them. It took about two weeks for the order to arrive and then I went to work, creating the piece.

Opposite page: ‘Birth, Living, Letting Go’ PIA+ acrylic, sparkles on plexiglass, Nicolee

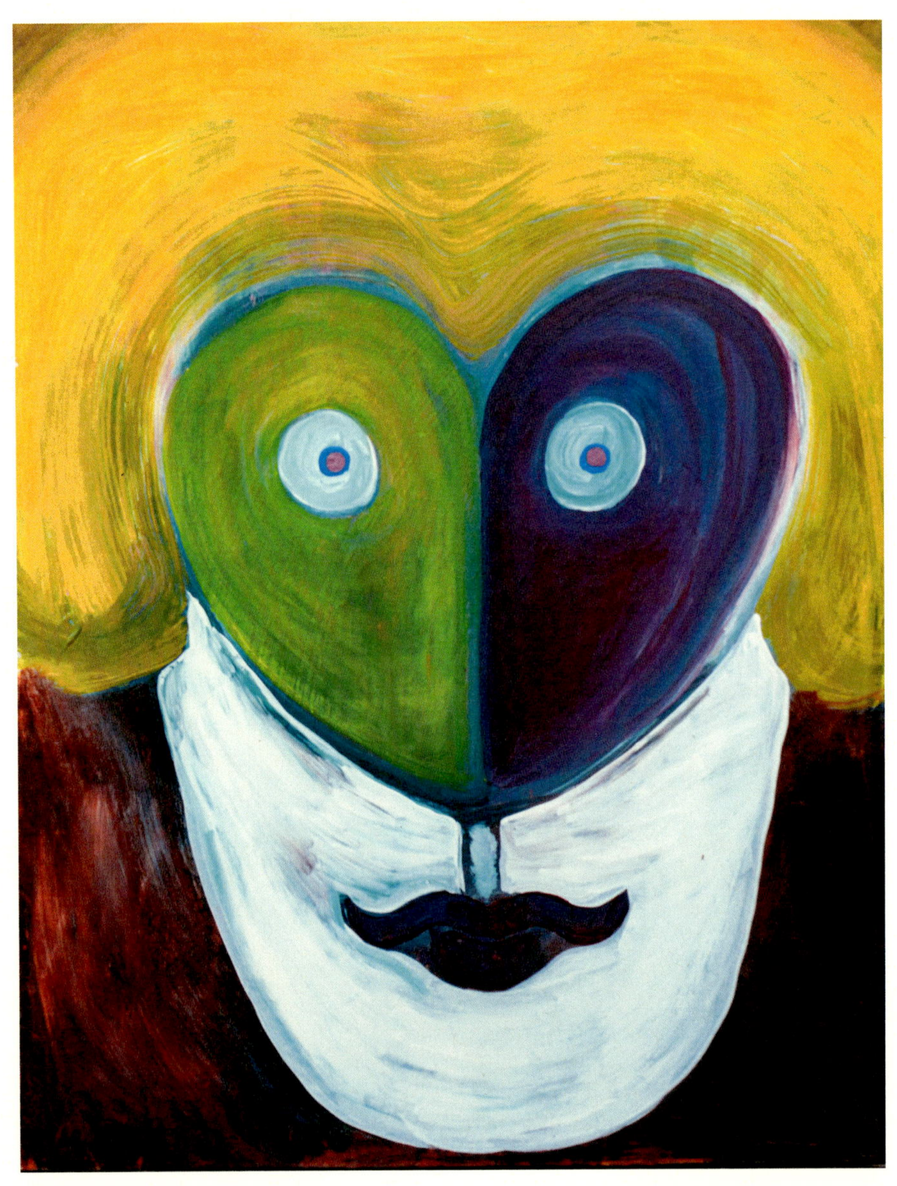

'Heart Mask' is a PIA that looked a lot like the finished piece above. I liked the image, but the colors needed to be worked with—the piece was completed at another time, which is why it is PIA+. Some revised PIA are actually PIA that are 95% completed in one session, but as they are worked on at another time, they are PIA+. There's an integrity in differentiating between the two as the original PIA is not preconceived; it emerges out of the living moment, complete. PIA+ is worked on, evaluated, adjusted over time.

Opposite page: 'Heart Mask' PIA+ acrylic on canvas, Nicolee

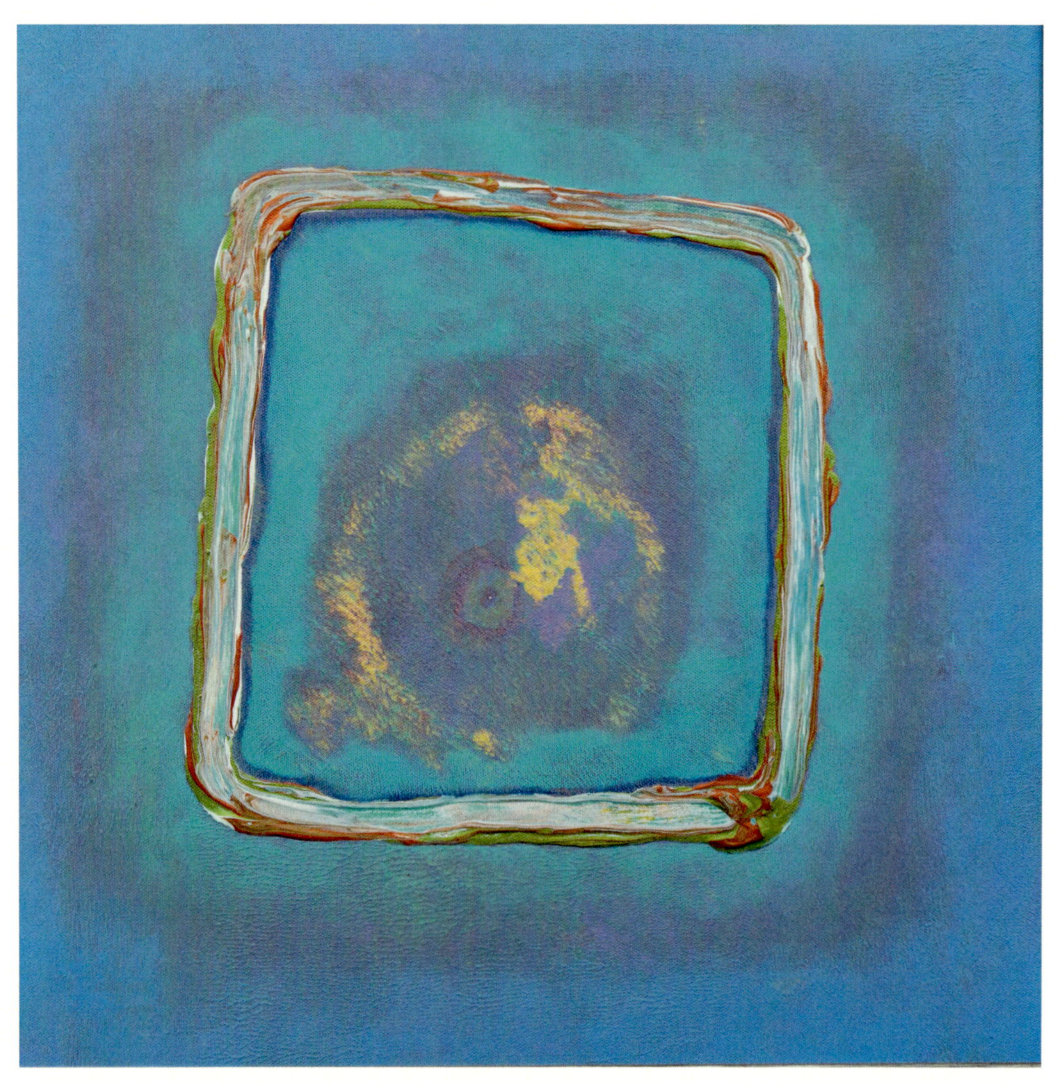

'Hubble View' began as PIA on a new, fresh canvas. Out of the creative flow this image emerged. I later worked on it for months until the colors and the images created a feeling of depth. When I look at 'Hubble View,' I feel I'm being pulled through a window into a distant part of the universe. Since I was a child, I've felt a deep connection to the cosmos. When photographs of the earth first appeared in print and on TV, I was filled with awe and wonder at how earth is held in the dark sky—how everything on this jewel-like globe is co-existing.

Opposite page: 'Hubble View', PIA+ acrylic on canvas, Nicolee

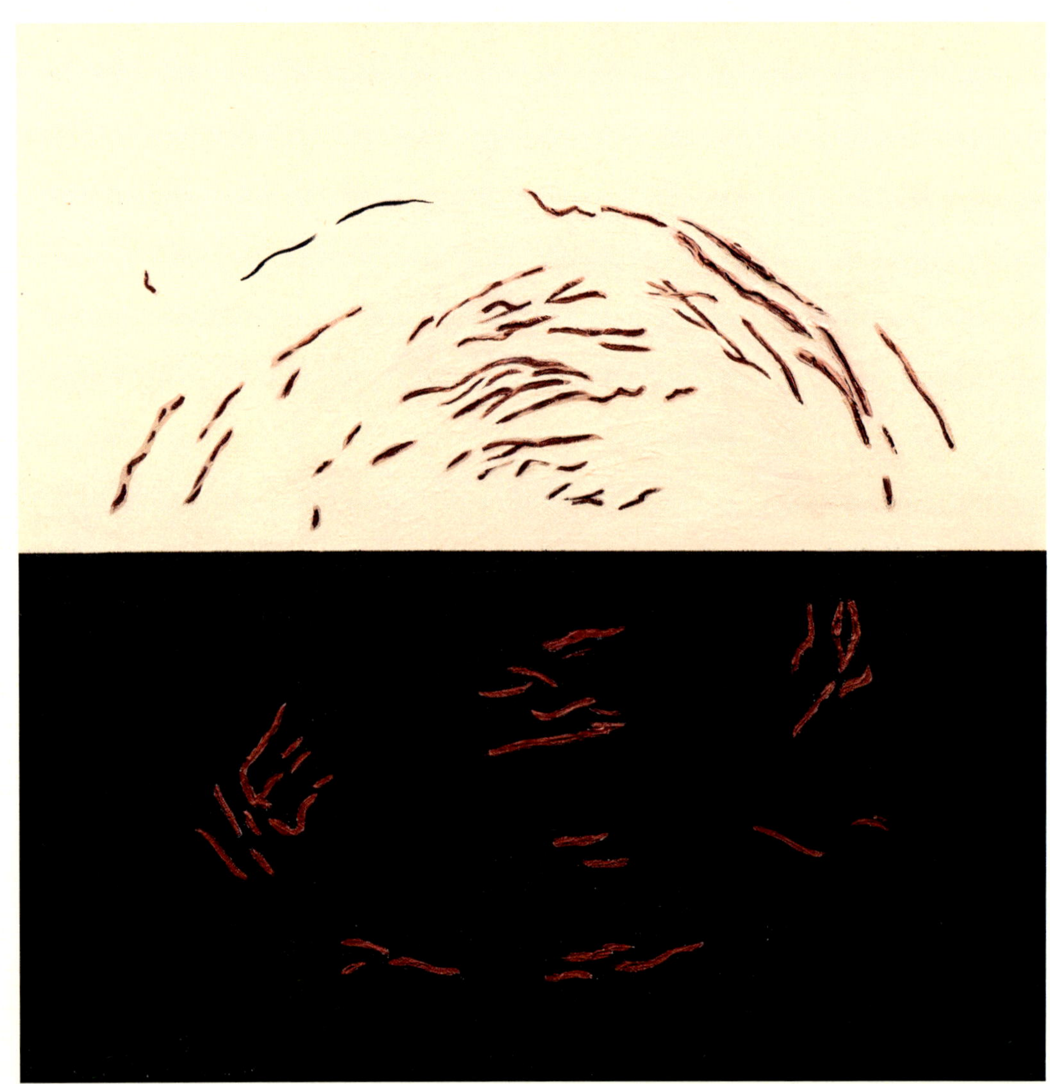

'Moving Balance' began as PIA on a fresh canvas. Red squiggly lines emerged moving in a circle between the dark and the light. As I needed a richer shade of black paint, I put the piece aside and came back to it at a later time. Returning to it, I wanted the line between the light and dark areas to be very defined and used masking tape to create the delineation. The photo on the opposite page is not as white as the piece, but it's close enough. There's a definite difference between what's in the dark area and what's in the light area—but they flow one to the other in a balanced, moving whole. What's hidden from awareness in the dark exerts its influence, regardless.

Opposite page: 'Moving Balance' PIA+ acrylic on canvas, Nicolee

Limp,
Tossed about by nature's breathing,
When not too busy or indifferent
To spare me even a breath.
Cold, exposed to elements attracted more
Ignored, eating the meals tossed by
"empty" ghosts, glittering shells,
begging bowls filled with nails
and crosses.
The winter cold and snow freeze my
very foundation,
sleet starches the very flow of me
and makes of my heart a
cold, icy thing dressed
in fearful shivers.
Cars whiz by en route to their
emergencies
while I flail my prayers, my
hurts, my forgottenness to the darkness.
Sirens scream, horns blast,
onlookers curse the noise but love
the adventure of it all.
Bright lights shine satin upon
patches of still clean snow
but all I see are crusty,
dirty dog-peed stains
carelessly allowed by
angry mongrels.
I'm left endlessly fluttering,
reaching for what?

a rainbow over there
offering some hope,
some beauty to my world of
beggars, hustlers, "thieves"
Who have stolen the dance
that was once mine?
Limp,
the heavy flag
has hidden my jewels
in locked closets only to be
displayed on special
holidays.What's next, Valentine's Day?

'Limp' PIA+ poem by Vivienne L. Lund

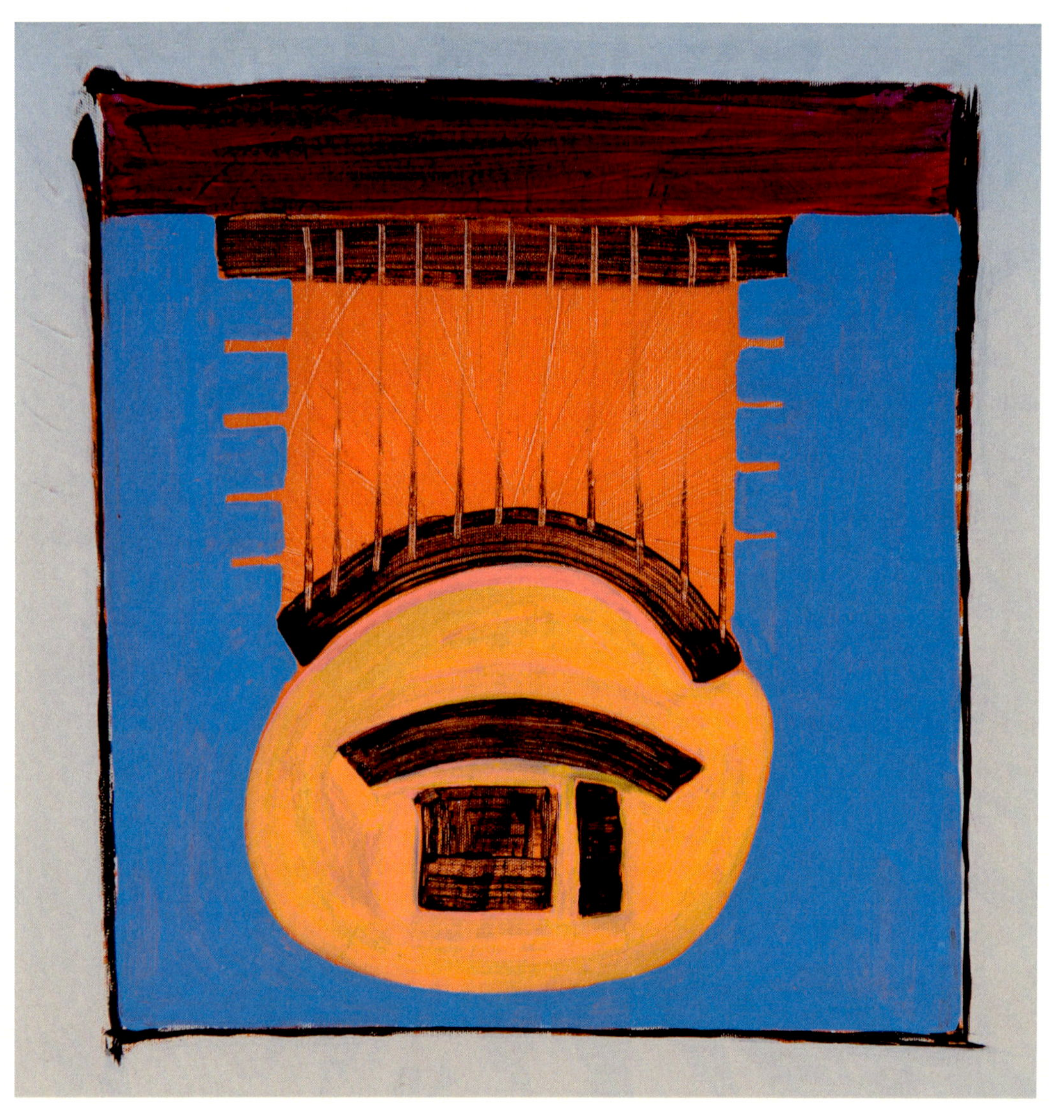

'Suspended' was a creative flow that emerged from PIA that surprised me when I looked at it. The image continues to fascinate me—there's a feeling of a weighty, golden, circular shape containing black lines and a blackish square, yet it's suspended. I'm waiting for it to drop, but it doesn't. The shade of blue was added at a later time as well as the maroon area on top. Sometimes I feel the gold ball would bounce if it were released.

Opposite page: 'Suspended' PIA+ acrylic on canvas, Nicolee

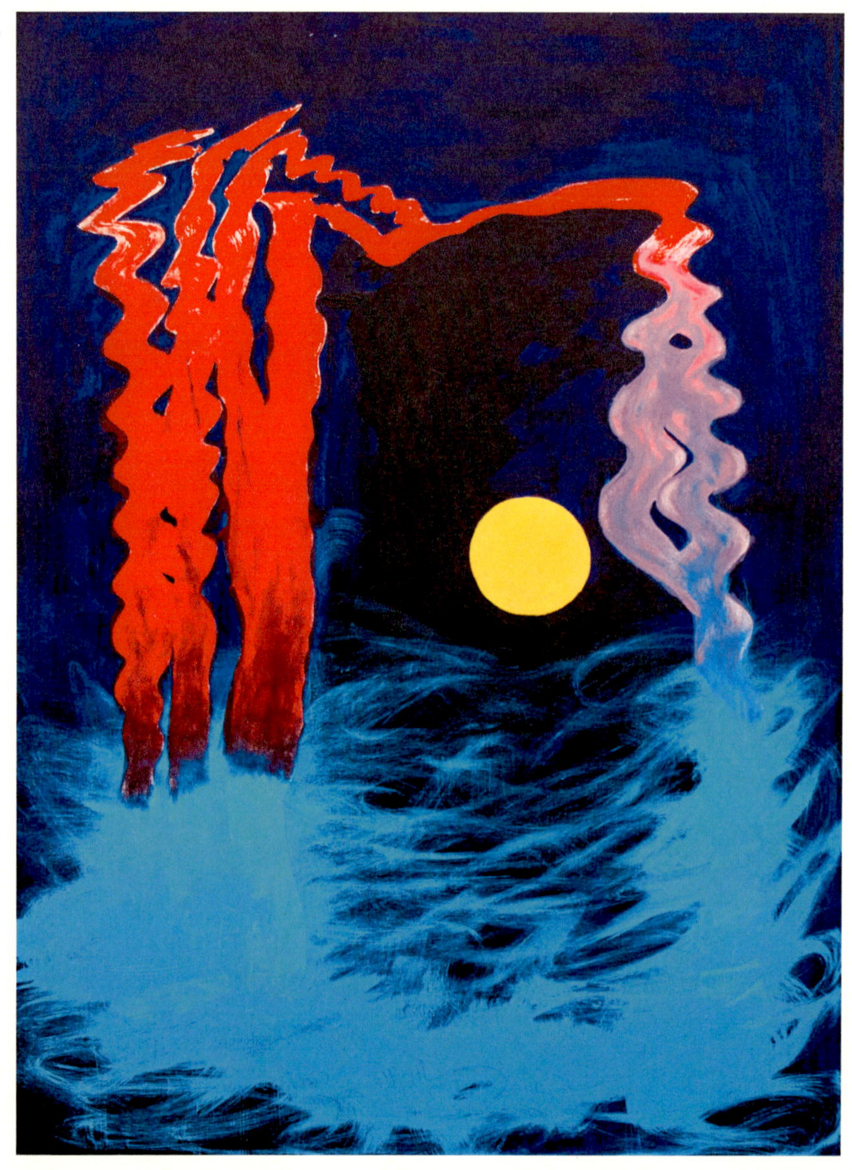

While I was practicing PIA, the sound of a water spigot repeated over and over while my neighbor's lawn was being watered. Beneath everything else that was arising in awareness in PIA, the sound of water was so constant that a creative flow captured the sound in form—thus the name 'Water Dance.' Later, when I looked at it, I wanted a darker shade of blue-black for the background and a more yellow moon. As these colors were added, more adjustments were needed until I felt in my body that the piece was finished. I particularly like this PIA+ as, for me, it's so direct and simple.

Opposite page: 'Water Dance' PIA+ acrylic on a large canvas, Nicolee

CONCLUSION

As everything is constantly emerging and interconnected, there is no real conclusion to what we create; rather, we are living in and engaged with a continual flow from one experience to the next. In that sense there is no beginning and no end. Yet clearly, if one is painting or playing music, expressing movement or writing, there is a finished product that emerges from our effort. But if we look very closely, that end is a new beginning.

I began this book with a section of Dogen Zenji's "Being Time" (Uji) to illuminate the *Arte of Now: Practice of Immediacy in the Arts.*™ Dogen, one of the seminal figures in Japanese Zen, skillfully expresses and captures several essential elements of PIA:

> "Things do not hinder each other, just as moments do not hinder one another."
> "Each moment is all being, is the entire world."
> "Reflect now whether any being or any world is left out of the present moment."
> "See each thing in this entire world as a moment of time."

Penetrating these teachings contributed to my understanding of the nature of life and the transformative power of practicing with each moment as inherently equal, whole, and complete. Nothing is missing and nothing is repeated. And at the same time, from our everyday perspective, each moment continually flows to the next. As such, when PIA entered my world in its unusual way, there was something so familiar about it, if I could only tap into the transformative power of what PIA was about creatively. Once I discovered this through the five simple directions and the *voice of PIA*, my creativity was liberated, and my hope is that sharing PIA could be a resource for your creative exploration and expression.

Some of what I have found in my creative journey with PIA is courage I didn't know I had, learning to trust creative flow, trusting myself to let go of knowing, deeply opening to not knowing, and creating space to nourish my creativity. We are on this immensely diverse, creative planet for such a short time; I hope you will take advantage of the creative gifts you have to bring forth.

Appendix: PIA and Revised PIA: Dates of Composition

PIA

Robert Althouse

(https://althouseart.com)

Swirls	PIA 2015
Abstract	PIA 2015

Joan Hoeberichts

Black Rose	PIA 2000

Annie Pirruccello

Eyes All Over	PIA 2011
The Body of Pain	PIA 2011
What's Happening Now	PIA 2014

Vivienne L. Lund

Limp	PIA+ 2015

Nicolee

Star Eye	PIA 1999
Chinese Lantern	PIA 2000
Moving	PIA 2001
Spears	PIA 2002
Journeying	PIA 2003
Promise to Mother Earth	PIA 2003
Word Fence	PIA 2003
Woman Dancing	PIA 2003
A Way Through	PIA 2004
Mandala	PIA 2004
Mask	PIA 2007
Birth	PIA 2008
Alien Communication	PIA 2009
Tears	PIA 2010
The Genie	PIA 2012
Dancing Paper	PIA 2012
Flowing	PIA 2012
Rising	PIA 2013
PI	PIA 2014
Wings	PIA 2014
Popeye Swallow the Universe	PIA 2014
Red Moon	PIA 2016

Revised PIA (PIA +)

Nicolee

Shaman's dream	PIA+ 2004
Untangling	PIA+ 2006
Suspended	PIA+ 2006
Heart Mask	PIA+ 2011
Hubble View	PIA+ 2011
Water Dance	PIA+ 2013
Cow Jumps Over the Moon	PIA+ 2014
Moving Balance	PIA+ 2014
Beadwork	PIA+ 2003-15
Birth, Living, Letting Go	PIA+ 2015

Nicolee McMahon, Roshi, is a Dharma heir of Zen Master Taizan Maezumi, Roshi. She is a co-founder of the Three Treasures Zen Community in San Diego, CA. She is semi-retired but continues to co-lead retreats several times a year. She has been creative throughout her life, and after an unusual experience, she developed the *Practice of Immediacy in the Arts*® (PIA) She is married, and has two grown children, a stepson, and four grandchildren. She is semiretired as a Marriage and Family Counselor.

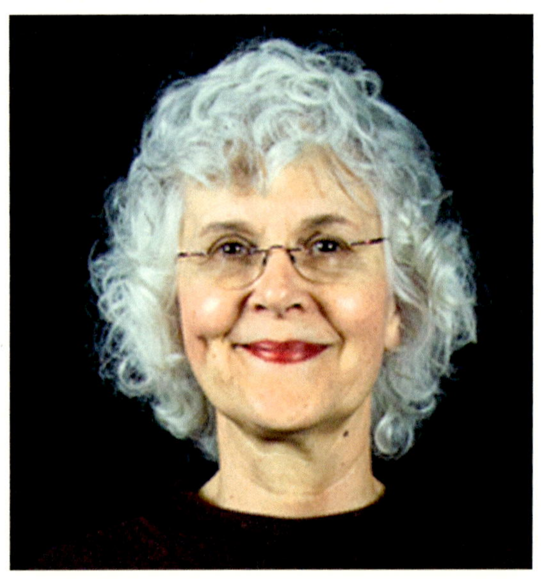